New Edition plus

Viewfinder

Topics

Australia and New Zealand

Down Under on Top

compiled and edited by
Martin Arndt and Karl Sassenberg

Langenscheidt

Berlin · München · Wien · Zürich
London · Madrid · New York · Warschau

Viewfinder

Topics – New Edition plus

Unterrichtsmaterialien für die Sekundarstufe II

Australia and New Zealand

Down Under on Top

Herausgeber:
Prof. em. Dr. Dr. h.c. mult. Peter Freese

Autoren:
Dr. Martin Arndt
StD Karl Sassenberg

Projekt-Team:
Dr. Martin Arndt, Münster
Prof. Dr. Mita Banerjee, Siegen
David Beal, M. A., Bochum
Cornelia Becker, Bremen
Dr. Peter Dines, Cert. Ed., Ludwigsburg
Prof. Dr. Hanspeter Dörfel †
Prof. Dr. Sabine Doff, München
Dr. Claudia Drawe, Essen
OStR Dieter Düwel, Castrop-Rauxel
Prof. em. Dr. Dr. h.c. Dr. h.c. Peter Freese, Paderborn
Dr. Carin Freywald †
Dr. Christine Gottstein-Strobl, Eichstätt
Jennifer von der Grün, B. A., Dortmund
OStR Ulrich Imig, Wildeshausen
OStR Reimer Jansen, Oyten-Sagehorn
Dr. Michael Mitchell, M. A., Reken und Warwick
Prof. Dr. Michael Porsche, Paderborn
Dr. Peter-J. Rekowski, Kirchhain
StD Peter Ringeisen, M. A., Amberg
StD Karl Sassenberg, Münster
StD Dr. Annegret Schrick, Essen
OStR Ekkehard Sprenger, Kiel
StR Susanne Stadler, Wiesbaden
OStD Dr. Dietrich Theißen †
Prof. Dr. Laurenz Volkmann, Jena
Philip Wade, M. A., Cert. Ed., Amberg

Verlagsredaktion: Dr. Beatrix Finke

Visuelles Konzept: Barbara Slowik, Atelier S., München

Layout und Produktion: kaltnermedia GmbH, Bobingen

www.langenscheidt.de/viewfinder

Umwelthinweis: Gedruckt auf chlorfrei gebleichtem Papier.

Druck: Mediengruppe Universal, München

Printed in Germany
ISBN: 978-3-526-51038-3

10010

Contents

* Title provided by the editors

Australia –

When you are celebrating Christmas or New Year's Eve in the middle of summer, when the water runs down the sink the other way round, and it's not the North Star but the Southern Cross that points the way at night you know you are "Down Under", where things are not upside down but, nevertheless, quite different.

A cattle station

Australia is 24 times larger than the British Isles or Germany. Remote cattle farms in the Outback are so vast that helicopters are used to round up the herds. One ranch is the size of Belgium.

Ayers Rock – Uluru

Uluru (or Ayers Rock) is sacred to the Australian Aborigines. It is about 550 million years old. The Aborigines have lived in Australia for at least 40,000 years. The first white settlers arrived in 1788.

The "Three Sisters" rock formation in the Blue Mountains

Eleven of the world's most poisonous snakes live in Australia and 3,000 people are bitten by snakes every year.

Eighty per cent of Australia's 22 million people (including the 200,000 Aborigines) live in cities mainly along the fertile coast between Brisbane and Adelaide.

Down Under on Top

Sydney Opera House

Bondi Beach, Sydney

The Great Barrier Reef

Australia is flat. The highest peak, Mount Kosciousko, is only 7,310 feet (2,230 metres) high. In the deserts temperatures can reach a blistering 175 degrees F. Over 2,000 kms of coral make the Great Barrier Reef the world's largest living phenomenon. It is so big that it can be seen from outer space.

Waltzing Matilda

The unofficial Australian national anthem

Once a jolly swagman camped by a billabong
Under the shade of a coolibah tree.
And he sang as he watched and waited till his billy boiled
"Who'll come a-waltzing Matilda with me?"

Chorus: Waltzing Matilda, waltzing Matilda,
You'll come a-waltzing Matilda with me.

Down came a jumbuck to drink at the billabong.
Up jumped the swagman and grabbed him with glee.
And he sang as he put that jumbuck in his tucker-bag
"You'll come a-waltzing Matilda with me!"
Chorus

Up came the squatter riding on his thoroughbred.
Up came the troopers, one, two, three.
"Where's that jolly jumbuck, you've got in your tucker-bag?
You'll come a-waltzing Matilda with me!"
Chorus

Up jumped the swagman and sprang into the billabong.
"You'll never take me alive!" said he.
And his ghost may be heard as you pass by that billabong
"Who'll come a-waltzing Matilda with me!"
Chorus

1 "The Whites' Arrival" *

Captain Arthur Phillip was commissioned as the first Governor of New South Wales. He set sail on May 13th, 1787 from Portsmouth with 11 vessels, being the First Fleet's commander. He arrived in New South Wales with 717 convicts (180 females) guarded by 191 marines under 19 officers. The naval officer, First Lieutenant William Bradley (1758–1833), belonged to the First Fleet serving on the "Sirius". He wrote a journal and a diary on his voyage to New South Wales. He was also a water colourist (see e.g. his painting of Port Jackson from January 1788: http://www.sl.nsw.gov.au/discover_collections/history_nation/terra_australis/journals/index.html). Immediately after reaching Port Jackson he began a series of surveys of the Sydney Harbour Coastline. His main interest were the Aboriginals, whose appearance and behaviour he studied extensively and described in his journal.

Excerpt from the *Diary of Lieutenant* ***Bradley Friday***, 30th May 1788 (http://firstfleet.uow.edu.au/index.html)

Scene near the River Darling

"We saw several of the natives on the high land. They were gathering a kind of fruit which they soaked in water & sucked. On our return to the Cove where we landed, we found a native in a tree gathering a fruit of the size of a small pine, & of a beautiful pale yellow. He got it by fixing a four-pronged spear over the stalk & twisting them off. It had a sweet taste. We found 2 children, a boy & a girl, near the tree in which the man was. The children did not appear frightened when we took hold of them. The girl's fingers were complete as were the boy's teeth. When the man had got a good quantity of this spungy fruit, he, with the children, walked along the beach & sat down by the side of a pool of fresh water, to which place we followed him. They eat or rather sucked the whole of what they had gathered, frequently dipping them in the water. They then returned to the place where we first met with them. They eagerly accepted of a gull which we gave them. On our return to the Sirius we found that some of the natives had been alongside and examined the outside of the ship with great attention, particularly the figure. They appeared to be the same that visited the ship some days before, as they had been shaved. They landed at the Observatory Point, stopped a short time & went up the Harbour. Capt Campbell, going to the S. W. arm with boats to bring down rushes for thatching his house, on landing at the place where 2 convicts had been left with a tent for the purpose of cutting those rushes, he found the tent but not the men. Finding some blood near the tent, they followed it to the mangrove bushes, where they found both men dead & laying at some distance from each other. One of them had 3 spears in him & one side of his head beat in. The other man had no apparent wound but a blow to the forehead."

Vocabulary

9 to soak (v.): to make s.th. completely wet – **10 to suck** (v.): to take liquid into your mouth – **15 four-pronged spear** (n.): a spear having four forks/hooks – **15 stalk** (n.): a long narrow part of a plant that supports leaves, fruits or flowers – **21 spungy** (n.): old spelling for "spongy", i.e.: soft and full of holes that contain air or liquid like a sponge – **24 eat:** here: ate – **28 gull** (n.): a large common black and white sea bird that lives near the sea – **39 Observatory Point** (n.): a special building from which scientists watch the moon, stars, weather etc – **41 rush** (n.): a type of tall grass that grows in water, often used for making baskets – **41 to thatch** (v.) – to build a roof with dry vegetation such as straw or water reed – **45 mangrove** (n.): a tropical tree that grows in or near water and grows new roots from its branches

Explanations

Intro: Sirius (n.): a flagship of the First Fleet, named after the brightest star in the nighty sky – **7 high land** (n.): also: highland, a region which is part of the Great Dividing Range (Eastern Highlands) in North-Eastern Queensland, Australia. It starts northeast of Melbourne and heads east to the New South Wales border. – **11 Cove** (n.): a part of the coast where the land curves round so that the sea is partly surrounded by land

Awareness

1 Have you ever made the experience of meeting people whose behaviour seemed strange to you? How did you react?
2 How would you prepare an excursion into an unknown territory?

Comprehension

3 What, in particular, aroused Bradley's attention?
4 What remains unknown from the story?

Analysis

5 The text is classified as a diary. Is the style of writing typical of this text-type?

Opinion

6 Imagine that you belonged to the group of natives. What would you tell your co-villagers in the evening?

Projects

7 What were the people like who founded the white settlement in Australia two hundred years ago?
8 Find out how many prisoners were convicted for murder and how many were transported for life.
9 Write a biographical report on Mary Ann Wade who was on the Second Fleet and one of the youngest convicts ever to be transported to Australia.

References: On the Whites' Arrival and the first encounters with the Aboriginals
http://www.janesoceania.com/australia_aboriginal_whitesettlers
Description of the First Fleet: http://firstfleet.uow.edu.au

2 Kate Grenville

"First Encounters" *

Australian novelist Kate Grenville was born in Sydney in 1950. She spent seven years in Europe and the USA working and studying and holds degrees from different universities. Her books have won several literary awards, among them the Orange Prize and the Commonwealth Writers' Prize. "First Encounters" is a passage taken from her most recent novel *The Secret River*, which deals with the settlement of New South Wales by a population of exiled British "criminals". – Kate Grenville, *The Secret River* (Edinburgh: Canongate Books, 2006), pp. 201–204.

Plot Outline

The protagonist William Thornhill, an illiterate Thames bargeman, grew up in the slums of London at the turn of the 19th century. He was caught stealing lumber but luckily for him, a life sentence in the penal colony of New South Wales saved him from the gallows. With his wife, Sal, and a growing number of children, Thornhill in 1806 was transported to the colony to live a convict's life of servitude near the banks of the Hawkesbury River. Life was difficult, but through hard work and initiative the

Thornhills slowly got ahead. William became a free man with his own claim to the savage land where he raised a hut and planted corn. As he struggled with the wilderness, Thornhill realized that the British were not the first to make New South Wales their home. The land had been part of the territory of the Darug people for perhaps forty thousand years. They had not left fences or roads or houses, but they lived on that land and used it.

Something made him turn. Behind him was a group of men standing together watching. They had arrived so quietly they might have risen up out of the ground. There were six of them, or perhaps eight, or ten. Something about the way their skins were shadows among the shadows of the trees made it hard to see them straight.

In London William Thornhill counted as a big man, but these men made him feel small. They were as tall as he was, their shoulders sinewy but powerful, their chests defined with pads of muscle. Each held a few spears, the lengths of wood shifting like insects' feelers.

He stood legs apart, his heavy new boots planted on the ground. He imagined the way he looked to them: his mysterious clothes, his face shadowed under his hat.

It seemed important to act the part of host. That way, they were his guests. He made himself hail them in a jovial way, looking them right in the face, as if they were dogs that would bite if they caught the scent of fear.

Good-day to you gentlemen, he called. *How are you this fine day?*

He heard his words evaporate, thin and silly, into the air, and was glad that Ned and Dan were not with him to hear. He felt something hot in his chest: anger? Or was it fear?

At home in the bush (19th century)

He wished he had the gun.

A bird began a long tweetling somewhere in the trees and the humming in the grass swelled and faded, swelled and faded. A stick fell in the fire with a soft collapsing sound.

A haze of steam was starting to come up from the place in the coals where the snake was cooking, and a good greasy smell was wafting over to him, like nothing so much as a nice fat mutton chop. He found himself wondering if a yard of serpent might not be such a bad dinner.

Cat got your tongues, he said. *You black buggers?* As if this was a signal, they came towards him, moving in that loose-kneed way they had, the spears easy in their hands. One – the same grey-beard he had slapped the first day – separated himself from the others and came right up to Thornhill, reaching out and placing a long black hand on his forearm. Authority radiated from this naked old man like heat off a fire. A stream of words began to come out of his mouth.

Thornhill forced himself to break the spell. *Very good, you old bugger,* he said, his voice harsh, cutting across the flow. *Now you listen.* He bent down and with a twig drew marks on the dust: a curving line that was the river, and a tidy square representing his own hundred acres. *This mine now. Thornhill's place.*

The man stared at him.

You got all the rest, Thornhill said. He could hear his voice getting louder. *You got the whole blessed rest of it, mate, and welcome to it.* But his words seemed to flow past the man as if they mattered as little as a current of air. He had not noticed before how white the white part of the man's eyes were. He wondered if it was that, the darkness of the skin against the whiteness of the eyes, that made his eyes seem to be lit from within.

The old man took a step towards the fire and from one of the bark dishes picked something up: a cluster of the daisy-roots, six or eight narrow tubers dangling from the stem. He pointed at the roots and spoke again. Finally he took a bite of one of them. Chewed, swallowed, nodded. Even with the words as meaningless to Thornhill as the cry of a bird, he understood. The man snapped off a finger of root and held it out to Thornhill. The flesh was translucent, glassy, crisp-looking, something in the nature of a radish.

But Thornhill did not intend to eat. *Kind of you, old boy.* That was a joke that had not lost its savour. *But you can keep your radishes.* He looked again at the thing on the man's brown-seamed pink palm. *Monkey food, I would call that, mate, but good luck to you.*

The man was vehement now. He was explaining something in detail. He turned and pointed towards the river-flats, holding up the bundle of roots. There seemed to be a question in his voice now, a phrase repeated, as if he wanted agreement.

Yes, mate, Thornhill said. *You can keep your monkey's balls that you like so much.* The old man said something, loud and sharp, and Thornhill recognised the same phrase.

He longed for words.

It seemed that the old man was ready to wait all day for an answer.

We'll stick to our victuals, mate, you stick to yours, Thornhill said. He met the man's eyes and nodded. The old man gave a curt nod back.

A conversation had taken place. There had been an inquiry and an answer. But what inquiry, which answer?

They stared at each other, their words between them like a wall.

Vocabulary

9 sinewy (adj.): a sinewy person has a thin body and strong muscles – **32 tweetling** (n.): a short high sound of a small bird – **38 to waft** (v.): to move through the air (especially of smells) – **39 mutton** (n.): meat of a (mature) sheep – **40 yard of serpent** (n.): a piece of a snake about 90 cm long – **42 Cat got your tongues:** Have you lost your tongue? (used to ask s.o. why they are not talking) – **42 buggers** (n.): here: Thornhill's humorous term for the men – **51 spell** (n.): here: magic of the moment – **59 blessed** (adj.): here: blasted – **69 bark** (n.): outer covering of a tree – **72 tuber** (n.): fleshy underground stem of a plant (such as the potato) – **84 savour** (n.): here: the power to excite interest

Explanations

26, 27 Ned, Dan: Thornhill's servants; as a free man Thornhill was allowed to pick some men from the convict newcomers who had to serve him as farmhands – **45 grey-beard**: Thornhill's name for the leader of the Aborigines, whom he had slapped on the shoulder a couple of days ago

Awareness

1 Use the internet to find the meanings of the following words and say which come from Australian Aboriginal languages.

barramundi	*billabong*	*boomerang*	*cockatoo*
coolibah	*corroborree*	*didgeridoo*	*dugong*
kangaroo	*koala*	*wallaby*	*wombat*

Comprehension

2 Who are the two main figures dominating the scene? Describe them and explain the problem they have.

3 What is Thornhill trying to do in this passage?

4 Why does he refuse to eat?

Analysis

5 Describe the setting of the scene and explain how the writer creates an uneasy atmosphere.

6 Show that Thornhill's attitude towards the Aborigines is ambivalent.

7 At the end of the text the narrator says: "They stared at each other, their words between them like a wall." Explain the meaning of this simile.

8 What is the effect of the author's notation of direct speech?

Opinion

9 Do you think the men would have come to an agreement if they had spoken the same language? Give reasons for your view. You may also consider the present relationship between white Australians and Aborigines.

10 Why do you think is it so important for Thornhill to own a piece of land?

Project

11 Gather information about early European explorers of Australia and find out why some of them starved to death.

James Cook (1728–1779): *cf. Info Box on p. 10*

Info

Who are the Aborigines?

Aborigine family as seen by a 19th century painter

Aborigines are Australia's indigenous people. They came originally from somewhere in Asia and have been resident in Australia for at least 40,000 years. The first arrived at a time when the sea level was lower and there was an almost continuous land bridge between Asia and Australia. Traditionally the Aborigines were hunter-gatherers who grew no crops and did not domesticate animals and so were completely dependent on their natural environment.

In 1770, at the time of James Cook's first landing, there were about 300,000 (estimates differ) Aborigines who occupied the entire continent, divided into 500–600 distinct groups. 200 different languages were spoken and we may assume that most Aborigines were bilingual or multilingual.

Most of the year people lived dispersed into small nomadic groups or bands, a band consisting of several families, and moved about a well defined territory or "estate" in search of food and water. They were intimately acquainted with all the country within their range of movement and could read the ground like a map.

3 Kevin Rudd

"Apology to Australia's Indigenous Peoples" *

On 13 February 2008, the newly elected Prime Minister Kevin Rudd apologised on behalf of the government to the Aboriginal People of Australia for the grief and suffering inflicted on them by the laws and policies of former governments. The speech – Rudd's first speech as Prime Minister – was broadcast on all television networks and viewed on big screens in public places all over Australia. It was also shown to children in school and is regarded as a landmark in Australian history. – The Prime Minister of Australia, Media Center, Speech: http://www.pm.gov.au/node/5952.

[...] To the Stolen Generations, I say the following: as Prime Minister of Australia, I am sorry.

On behalf of the Government of Australia, I am sorry. On behalf of the Parliament of Australia, I am sorry. And I offer you this apology without qualification.

We apologise for the hurt, the pain and suffering we, the parliament, have caused you by the laws that previous parliaments have enacted. We apologise for the indignity, the degradation and the humiliation these laws embodied.

We offer this apology to the mothers, the fathers, the brothers, the sisters, the families and the communities whose lives were ripped apart by the actions of successive governments under successive parliaments. In making this apology, I would also like to speak personally to the members of the Stolen Generation and their families: to those here today, so many of you; to those listening across the nation – from Yuendumu, in the central west of the Northern Territory, to Yabara, in North Queensland, and to Pitjantjatjara in South Australia.

I know that, in offering this apology on behalf of the government and the parliament, there is nothing I can say today that can take away the pain you have suffered personally. Whatever words I speak today, I cannot undo that. Words alone are not that powerful. Grief is a very personal thing. I say to non-Indigenous Australians listening today who may not fully understand why what we are doing is so important, I ask those non-Indigenous Australians to imagine for a moment if this had happened to you. I say to honourable members here present:

imagine if this had happened to us. Imagine the crippling effect. Imagine how hard it would be to forgive. But my proposal is this: if the apology we extend today is accepted in the spirit of reconciliation, in which it is offered, we can today resolve together that there be a new beginning for Australia. And it is to such a new beginning that I believe the nation is now calling us.

Australians are a passionate lot. We are also a very practical lot. For us, symbolism is important but, unless the great symbolism of reconciliation is accompanied by an even greater substance, it is little more than a clanging gong. It is not sentiment that makes history; it is our actions that make history. Today's apology, however inadequate, is aimed at righting past wrongs. It is also aimed at building a bridge between Indigenous and non-Indigenous Australians – a bridge based on a real respect rather than a thinly veiled contempt. Our challenge for the future is now to cross that bridge and, in so doing, embrace a new partnership between Indigenous and non-Indigenous Australians. Embracing, as part of that partnership, expanded link-up and other critical services to help the Stolen Generations to trace their families, if at all possible, and to provide dignity to their lives. But the core of this partnership for the future is to close the gap between Indigenous and non-Indigenous Australians on life expectancy, educational achievement and employment opportunities. This new partnership on closing the gap will set concrete targets for the future: within a decade to halve the widening gap in literacy, numeracy and employment outcomes and opportunities for Indigenous children, within a decade to halve the appalling gap in infant mortality rates between Indigenous and non-Indigenous children and, within a generation, to close the equally appalling 17-year life gap between Indigenous and non-Indigenous when it comes to overall life expectancy. [...]

Today the parliament has come together to right a great wrong. We have come together to deal with the past so that we might fully embrace the future. And we have had sufficient audacity of faith to advance a pathway to that future, with arms extended rather than with fists still clenched. So let us seize the day. Let it not become a moment of mere sentimental reflection.

A public apology

Let us take it with both hands and allow this day, this day of national reconciliation, to become one of those rare moments in which we might just be able to transform the way in which the nation thinks about itself, whereby the injustice administered to these Stolen Generations in the name of these, our parliaments, causes all of us to reappraise, at the deepest level of our beliefs, the real possibility of reconciliation writ large. Reconciliation across all Indigenous Australia. Reconciliation across the entire history of the often bloody encounter between those who emerged from the Dreamtime a thousand generations ago and those who, like me, came across the seas only yesterday. Reconciliation which opens up whole new possibilities for the future. [...]

Vocabulary

5 qualification (n.): here: reservation – **33 to extend** (v.): here: to offer – **77 whereby** (adv.): by means of which – **78 the injustice administered**: the injustice officially done – **81 writ large** (adj., literary): in a very clear strong form

Explanations

Intro: Kevin Michael Rudd (1957 –): 26th Prime Minister of Australia, member of the *Australian Labor Party (ALP)*. He won the federal election on 24 November 2007 and succeeded John Howard (*Liberal Party*) who was Prime Minister from 1996 to 2007. His term as a Prime Minister finished in June 2010 (see also p. 46). – **1 Stolen Generation(s)**: see p. 12 – **18ff. Yuendumu, Yabara, Pitjantjatjara**: Aboriginal settlements in the different states of Australia – **51 link-up**: name of different organisations which help to reunite separated Aboriginal families

Awareness

1 Collect information on the subject of political rhetoric. Find out the meaning of such terms as *assertion, euphemism, generalisation, hyperbole, parallelism, repetition* and *symbol.*

2 Who belongs to Australia's "Stolen Generation"? Find out what happened to these people.

Comprehension

3 Who are the addressees of this speech?

4 What does Kevin Rudd offer the Indigenous Australians beside his apology for past wrongs?

Analysis

5 Find out into which parts this extract from the speech can be divided. Explain how Rudd has organised his thoughts.

6 How does he try to create an atmosphere of mutual trust and make the Aborigines accept his apology?

7 What is the purpose of the last paragraph? Which rhetorical means does Rudd use here and to which effect?

Opinion

8 The speech was widely applauded by Indigenous and non-Indigenuos Australians. Imagine yourself as a member of the Stolen Generation and explain which passages you find especially moving. Decide if you would accept this apology.

9 One of the frequently asked questions in response to the speech was: "Why should we apologise when many Aboriginal people are actually better off because they were removed from dysfunctional families?" Discuss this question.

Projects

10 Canada's indigenous population shares some of the experiences of Indigenous Australians. Find out what happened from 1920 until early 1970 to Canadian First Nation children. What was the government's reaction to this "horrendous period of Canadian history" (United Church of Canada)?

11 Collect, select and present material illustrating differences and similarities between the "Americanisation of the American natives" and the treatment of native Australians by white governments.

12 Compare the films *Rabbit-Proof Fence* (2002) and *Australia* (2008) and explain in which way each of them deals with the problems of the Stolen Generation.

Info

The Stolen Generation

In 1995 the Government launched an inquiry into a tragic episode in Australian history – the practice of removing Aboriginal children from their families with the aim of assimilating them into Western culture. This practice went on throughout most of this century until the late 1960s. The report *Bringing them home* chaired by former High Court judge Sir Ronald Wilson told in heart-rending detail of the agony endured by Aboriginals as a result of Government policy. The policy was not just wrong, the report stated. It was 'genocidal': the policy's aim was the disappearance of Aborigines as a distinct group, and this was genocide, as defined in the Convention on Genocide ratified by Australia in 1949. A "Sorry Day" was held exactly a year after the publication of the report.

From: Educational Activities for National Sorry Day, Tuesday 26 May 1998, http://balaguaustralia.multiply.com/journal.

Tasks

1 Read at least one story from *Bringing them home*. It is available through http://www.austlii.edu.au/au/other/IndigLRes/stolen/index.html

2 You can also listen to interviews: http://www.nla.gov.au/apps/audiodelivery/ apps/?wicket:interface=:1.

3 Based on this information, set up a debate or a mock court to discuss questions such as: Were the various government policies to separate Indigenous children from their families genocide?
A full documentation of the above is available on pp. 600 to 648 of the same document. On the internet site: www.hreoc.gov.au see "Stolen children" section.

4

Anonymous

"Bush Boys" *

As a closer look at the map of Australia may reveal, there are not only places that clearly show the British influence (e.g. Darwin, Canterbury, Elizabeth, Derby, Queensland, Richmond, Stratford, New South Wales, Victoria, Windsor etc), but also some that seem to have a different background: e.g. Ballarat ('a pleasant resting place'), Briagolong ('men of the west'), Korumburra ("a blowfly") and Mallacoota ('a place of meeting') are derived from aboriginal words. The Australian continent has been inhabited by Aborigines for at least 40,000 years. They had immigrated from Southeast Asia and had probably entered Australia via Cape York peninsula. They mainly lived by food-gathering and hunting. When the Europeans colonised the continent in the 18th century, between 300,000 to 1,000,000 Aborigines were still alive. Some early visitors idealised them as the authentic and uncorrupted interpreters of the Book of Nature, but the majority of Whites tragically regarded them as barbarians, since they were incompetent to alter and redefine their concept of civilisation. Here two children of the Loritja Tribe in Central Australia react to their modern role as a tourist attraction. - Douglas Lockwood, ed., *We, The Aborigines* (Sydney: J. B. Books, McPherson's Printing Group, 1963), pp.189ff.

Out here at Angas Downs station, 150 miles south west of Alice Springs, life was always lonely and monotonous.

We were Children of the Sun, naked as the changeless blue sky, anonymous, friendless, wilderness waifs who were never likely to get their photographs in print.

But look at us now. We've both got shirts and shorts and big balloons. And The Boss here says he wants to put us in a book, whatever that might be.

Life changed for us recently when tourist companies began to exploit a lump of rock we have out this way.

Actually it's quite a big rock. In fact we are told it is the biggest single rock in the world.

The white people call it Ayers Rock, but to us and our Elders in the Loritja tribe it has always been Uluru. More than five miles around it at the base. Twelve hundred feet high. A huge monolith where our ancestors danced interminable corroborees with tribesmen who came from hundreds of miles away.

Many spirit people still live there: the serpent people, the mice women, the kangaroo rat men. It is a sacred place because of its importance as a living symbol of the things and the times that are dead.

Although The Rock is a sacred place it has never been secret or taboo. There are dozens of legends and myths concerning its origins. The geologists say that it was originally laid down as horizontal sandstone. Its present tilted position was caused by upheavals in Protozoic

Aborigine children with their grandmother

times when the great Central Australian fault planes occurred and formed the folding now apparent in the mountain ranges around Alice Springs.

That's what *they say*. But we know better. We know it was formed in The Dreamtime by our own culture heroes. And those big round holes in the cliff face. Why, surely everyone knows they were made by the spears of warriors who were attacking an enemy camped there.

We also know that a big aboriginal woman named Bularri lives inside the rock. Oh, yes, we know it is solid; nevertheless, she lives inside. Ask any of our tribesmen.

Among the enormous boulders at the base of The Rock there is one with a hole in it. This was made when it was pierced by a heavy spear – because the boulder at that time was being held aloft as a shield by an opposing tribesman.

Mutidjula rock-hole is important to us, because it was on this part of Uluru that the sacred serpent lived. The serpent saved the lives of thirsty people in times of drought; it was lured from its hiding place by cries of Kuka ... Kuka ... Kuka. As it came out it disgorged hundreds of gallons of water which flowed down to the perishing people below.

Now the tourists come in droves – four thousand of them in six months of this season.

Most of them are women. They leave Alice Springs before dawn in a big bus and drive through the mulga for three hundred miles before reaching Uluru after dark.

On the way they pass through Angas Downs. That's why we're wearing shirts, even if they are a size or so too large.

Our drab and monotonous lives have changed miraculously. They give us lollies and toys and balloons (we're just waiting for them to go so we can prick them on a spinifex bush) and they all take photographs.

In four years we estimate that we have posed at least ten thousand times. We think that next year we might charge professional models' fees.

And, oh, the questions! You'd never believe it.

'What's your name, sonny?'

'Do you live here?'

'Do you like it?'

'How old are you? Do you go to school? Do you have plenty to eat?'

One day when the bus came in we submitted as usual, but then decided to ask a few questions ourselves. We said to a middle-aged lady, 'What's your name, Missus?'

'Where do you live?'

'Do you like it there?'

'How old are you?'

'Do you go to school?'

'Do you have plenty to eat?'

She was very cross and said to her friends, 'What cheeky children!'

But why is it cheeky for us to ask these questions and polite for her to do so?

What *are* our names? Look, Mister, if you don't mind we'd prefer to remain anonymous. It's enough to have our privacy invaded like this, and to be photographed and questioned and prodded and patted on the head without getting our names in print.

Douglas Lockwood (1918–1980) was a famous Australian managing editor and writer who was born in Natimuk. He won several awards, e.g. the Advertiser Prize and the London Evening News Award in 1957 and the Walkley Award in 1958. He is known for his books *Crocodiles and Other People* (1959), *Fair Dinkum* (1960), *Life on the Daly River* (1961), *I, the Aboriginal* (1962), *We, the Aborigines* (1963), *The Front Door* (1968) and *My Old Mates and I* (1979). Lockwood belongs to those writers of the 20th century who wanted to really get to know the Aborigines and to present them as human beings rather than scientific phenomena.

Vocabulary

Intro: blowfly (n.): a common meat fly – **Intro: Aborigines**: see text 5 and Info Box p. 10 – **5 waif** (n.): a homeless person – **17 monolith** (n.): a single block of stone – **18 interminable** (adj.): endless – **18 corroboree** (n.): here: a warlike dance-drama with song of Australian Aboriginals, cf. explanations p. 21 – **28 tilted** (adj.): not in an upright position – **29 fault** (n.): a fracture in the earth's crust – **40 boulder** (n.): a large stone made smooth by erosion – **48 to lure** (v.): to attract by using a trick – **49 to disgorge** (v.): to pour forth, to eject – **52 in droves** (n.): in great numbers – **55 mulga** (n.): a wood of shrubby plants that are widespread in the drier parts of Australia – **60 drab** (adj.): dull, uninteresting – **68 sonny** (n.): young boy – **89 to prod** (v.): to stir s.o., to stimulate s.o.

Explanations

Intro: Cape York peninsula: a triangle of land about 90,000 square miles in extent, forming the northernmost part of Queensland – **Intro: Book of Nature**: philosophical term referring to the idea that in a pre-civilised world the meaning of nature and the cosmos was understandable to certain people who had a privileged knowledge – **Intro: Loritja Tribe** (n.): an Aboriginal tribe that mainly lived in Central Australia – **1 Angas Downs** (n.): a town named after the philanthropist and founder of South Australia, George Fife Angas (1789–1879) – **2 Alice Springs**: a town in the Northern Territory, situated on the Todd River – **4 Children of the Sun**: uncorrupt humans who are thought to be pure and innocent – **14 Ayers Rock** (n.): a giant monolith in southwestern Northern Territory, sacred to the Aboriginals; it reaches an altitude of 1,100 feet - **15 Uluru**: an Aboriginal word literally translated as 'the great pebble (rock)' - **33 Dreamtime**: In the mythology of (some) Aboriginals the word refers to the Golden Age when the first ancestors were created - See also text 5 and the Info Box on p. 19 - **38 Bularri**: an Aboriginal name - **45 Mutidjula**: an Aboriginal name - **63 spinifex bush** (n.): any of a genus of Australian grasses with thorny seeds or stiff sharp leaves

Awareness

1 Discuss why Australia has become a tourist attraction.

Comprehension

2 What animate beings do the Aboriginals believe in?
3 What groups of people do the Aboriginals have difficulty in understanding and whose world-view do they consider a threat to their culture?

Analysis

4 What stylistic devices are used in the Aboriginal boys' expression of antipathy towards the Whites?
5 Characterise in your own words the changes that the tourism industry has been responsible for and its effects on the Aboriginals' identity.

Opinion

6 Explain how you would react to tourists visiting your home country if they asked obviously silly or even derogatory questions.
7 What sort of questions would you as a tourist ask the boys?
8 Imagine you were one of the tourists and you heard about the boys' complaints – write a letter to them that explains your interest.
9 Discuss whether the tourism industry has a positive or a negative effect on bi-cultural understanding.

Project

10 Gather information on the way Australia is presented in various tourist catalogues. Compare the advertisements. You may also contact Qantas Airline (Frankfurt airport).

5 "The Birth of the Butterflies"

From an early age, storytelling plays a vital role in transmitting knowledge and wisdom. Stories are a way of uniting the members of a social group. Gathered around the camp fire in the evening, on an expedition to a favourite waterhole, or at a landmark of special significance, parents, elders or aunts and uncles use the stories as the first part of a child's education. The following story was narrated by the elders of a tribe in Arnhem Land in the Northern Territory of Australia. It vividly illustrates the close bond between the Aboriginals and their natural environment - a relationship which is based on what we in Europe usually call the mythology of their 'Dreamtime'.– http://www.janesoceania.com/australia aboriginal dreamtime/index1.htm.

Long ago in the Dreamtime, when the world was very young, all the birds and animals spoke the same language. So the Kookaburra could talk to the Wombat, and the wombat to the Emu, and the Eagle to the Koala. And at this time, all the birds and animals lived forever, no one ever died. None of the creatures knew about death because they had never seen it.

A cruiser (butterfly species from Queensland)

Then one morning, a young Cockatoo was playing high up in a tree. He called to the other animals, "Corock, corock, look at me, swinging on a branch!" The others looked up – he was very high. They watched him dance from branch to branch. Then, suddenly, he slipped and fell. All the way to the ground! With a loud 'whoomph' he landed on his head. The other animals rushed up and saw the Cockatoo lying very still. "What a good trick. Cockatoo!" "Will you show us?" "Didn't he look funny when he landed!" But the Cockatoo didn't move. Perhaps he was embarrassed and hiding his face in the sand. Or perhaps he was just having a sleep. They tried to wake him, but they couldn't. He just lay there.

Famous Australian birds: the cockatoo …

Then the wise old Wombat waddled up. He looked at the little Cockatoo lying there, his head to one side. The wombat took a good look at the Cockatoo. Then he felt his tiny body, and turned to the other animals, telling them that the Cockatoo had broken his neck. "What does that mean, Wombat?" "Yes, Wombat, what does that mean? Did the Spirits do it?" The old Wombat thought for a while. The Spirits must have done this. They must have done this for a reason, but what reason?

… and the kookaburra

The Wombat called a meeting under a big old gum tree in the sandy creek bed. All the animals came. The Snakes, the Crows, the Possums, the Emus, the Caterpillars, the Kangaroos – all the birds and animals. "Tell us about the Cockatoo.' 'Sssshh! Did you see him fall, Wombat?' 'Is he still there?"

While they were talking, the Spirits came and took the little Cockatoo up into the sky. As the animals looked up, they could see the little Cockatoo wafting away into the sky. When the animals saw this, they were even more puzzled. What had happened to the Cockatoo, and what were the Spirits going to do with him? This had certainly never happened before. Then the Wombat spoke, very slowly: "I think, I think that the Spirits have taken the Cockatoo up into the sky, so they can change him into something else."

The animals were confused, but they were also curious. Then the Possum said: "What if someone went up into the sky, and waited to see what the Spirits do with the little Cockatoo?" The wombat thought that this was an excellent idea – but who was to go? Wombat was certainly too old to be climbing around the sky. Anyway, it was nearly winter, and he had his burrow to fix.

He asked the Snakes. "Shhhh, not usss, not usss – we're too sssleepy." So he asked the Crows: "Coark, coark, well we'd like to, but..." So he asked the Kangaroos: "Don't send us, what about the Magpie Geese, they're always poking their noses into our business!" So he asked the Magpie Geese: "You only asked us because the Kangaroos said to."

The Wombat was stuck. None of the animals wanted to go. He understood. It did mean spending the whole winter there; it would be cold, and there would be no shelter. Ah well, he thought, we'll never find out.

Then the Caterpillars wriggled up: "What about us? We never get asked to do things. All of us could go together, then we can make our camp and spend the whole winter there. When it gets warm in the spring we will come back and tell you what has happened to the little Cockatoo!" The animals cheered: "Good old Caterpillars!" They would find out what happened to the little Cockatoo, even if it did mean spending the whole winter there. So the Caterpillars gathered, and in one huge wriggling cloud, went up into the sky. And all the other animals sat down to wait for the spring.

When the winter was nearly over, the Wombat called all the animals together. They agreed to send out a hunting party to look for the Caterpillars. The Snakes said they would go, but they found nothing. The next day, the Crows flew off to look, but no Caterpillars. Each day, a group of animals would go out, searching for the Caterpillars, and each day they would return with nothing.

Then, on the first warm day of spring, a pair of Dragonflies came rushing back to where the animals were camped. They were very very excited. "We have seen them! We have seen them! And they are different! They are returning with new bodies!" Then the Dragonflies flew off to bring the Caterpillars back to where the animals were camped. The animals waited. What would the Caterpillars look like?

Then they saw them. A beautiful parade of brightly coloured wings! Reds and blues, whites and yellows. The first Butterflies! As the Butterflies flicked and flitted, the animals realized that here was the proof that the spirits had given the Caterpillars a new and beautiful shape. They also realized that when the Spirits took the little Cockatoo, they took him so that they could give him a new shape, so that he could become a new creature. As the Butterflies settled in the trees, they made such a pretty sight that the old ones decided that this must always be so.

So, ever since then, the caterpillars spend winter hidden in cocoons, preparing for the change into their beautiful spring bodies, just as they did long ago in the Dreamtime.

A koala snoozing after his daily meal of eucalyptus leaves

Vocabulary

30 to waddle (v.): to walk with short steps, with your body moving from one side to another - **49 to waft** (v.): to drift; to float - **71 burrow** (n.): a passage in the ground made by an animal such as a rabbit or fox as a place to live; lair, shelter - **83 to wriggle up** (v.): to twist your body from side to side with small quick movements - **122 cocoon** (n.): a silk cover that young moths and other insects make to protect themselves while they are growing

Wombats can only be found in Australia

Explanations

3 kookaburra (n.): an Australian bird whose song sounds like laughter; it belongs to the family of Kingfishers (also known as the Laughing Jackasses of Australia). The bird inhabits woodland areas of eastern and south western Australia; his rolling, laughing call is one of the best-known sounds in the animal world. - **3 wombat** (n.): an Australian animal like a small bear whose young live in a pocket of skin on its body; it can be found in the bushes of Australia - **4 emu** (n.): the largest Australian bird, related to the ostrich, that can run very fast, but cannot fly: the emu is often associated with the native companion bird, and in myths about the origin of the sun the emu and the native companion are the cosmic actors who bring light to the Earth - **9 cockatoo** (n.): an Australian parrot with a lot of feathers on top of its head, easily recognisable by the showy crests and curved bill - **42 possum** (n.): one of various types of small furry and long-tailed animals that climb trees - **75 magpie goose** (n.): a waterbird species with black and white feathers, yellowish legs and a long tail - **103 dragonfly** (n.): a brightly-coloured insect with a long thin body and transparent wings which lives near water

Awareness

1 Collect information on the meaning of mythology (see e.g. http://www.janesoceania.com/australia_aboriginal_mythology1/index1.htm).

2 Which animals do you know that are typically Australian (see e.g. http://www.herpindiego.com/ATR2007-3.html) ?

Comprehension

3 Is there an idea in the text that makes you stop and think, or prompts questions? Identify the idea and explain your responses.

4 Does the text leave you with questions you would like to ask? If so, what are they?

5 Would you like to direct your questions at a particular character?

6 What questions would you like to ask the anonymous author?

Analysis

7 Examine the structure of the narrative by working on the connectives.

8 What may be the message and moral of the narrative?

Opinion

9 What emotions does the text invoke: laughter, tears, smiles, anger? Record some of your reactions.

10 Would you like to be one of the characters or have some of their personality traits? Which of the characters would you become, if you could? Why?

11 Would you like to read more Aboriginal narratives? Why or why not?

Projects

12 Some people assert that Aboriginal stories contain more ethics than all the writings of Charles Dickens or Peter Singer together. They refer e.g. to the narrative *Tiddelak, the Giant Frog* (for summaries see http://www.acra.org.au/culture/aboriginal-hunter/dreaming-stories/89-tiddalik-the-frog.html; http://www.homileticsonline.com; http://www.onlineopinion.com.au/view.asp?article=6277&page=0; http://www.hotkey.net.au/~acdn/Animation%20Workshop%202003.htm; for other stories see: http://www.gadimirrabooka.com/contents.php): What may they think of ?

13 Defend the Aboriginals' view of the world by writing an effective criticism of the dominant attitude of industrialised countries towards nature. You might consult internet resources, especially using terms like 'relations between humans and nature', 'ecology' and 'environmental ethics' (e.g. http://home.ca.inter.net/~greenweb/DE-Animals.html).

14 Work on the accusations raised against the Australian ex-Prime Minister Howard (e.g. http://www.aph.gov.au/Senate/committee/indigenousaffairs_ctte/submissions/sub15a.pdf).

15 What is meant by genocide? (see http://www.edwebproject.org/sideshow/genocide/convention.html; http://sites.google.com/site/aboriginalgenocide)

16 Would you sign the far-reaching "Complaint to the International Criminal Court" (ICC) over Australia and Aboriginal, Iraqi, Afghan & Climate Genocides" made by Dr Gideon Polya (http://climateemergency.blogspot.com/2008/02/formal-complaint-to-international.html)? Give reasons for your answer.

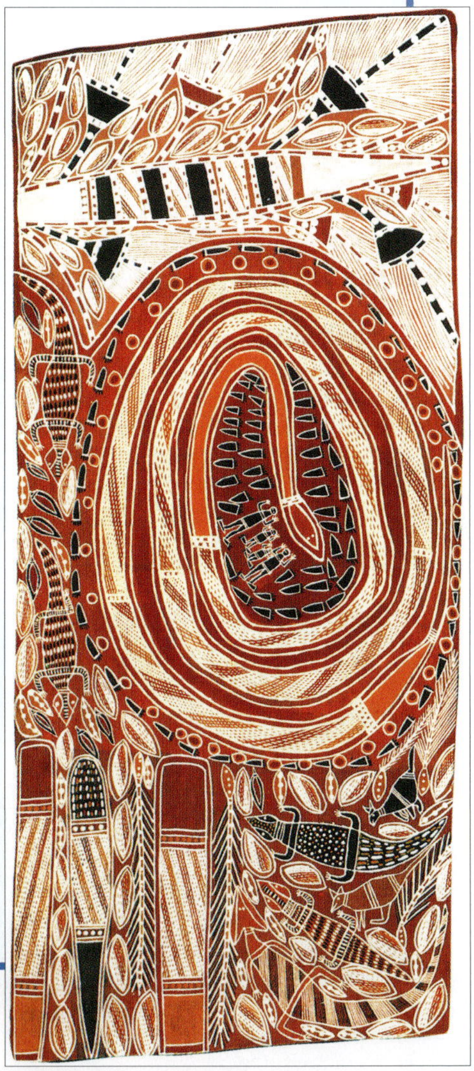

Aboriginal art: Rainbow serpent

Info

Dreamtime

As to all peoples in the world, religion is of great importance to the Aboriginals. According to their belief, all life as it is today – humans, animals, birds and fish – is part of one vast unchanging network of relationships which can be traced to the great spirit ancestors of the distant time (= Dreamtime). The term 'Dreamtime' is described as the 'time before time' or 'time of creation'. It is a mythological period of time during which the natural world was shaped by the actions of mythical beings who during the creation of the world moved across a barren land, hunting, camping, fighting and loving and in doing so shaped a featureless landscape. These ancestral beings made the ants, the emus, the crows, the possums, the wallabies, the kangaroos, the lizards, the goanna, the snakes and all the food and plants, the sun, the moon and the planets, the humans, tribes and clans. Some of the beings took the form of 'totemic' animals or human forms, changing and forming the world around us. These became sacred places, to be seen only by initiated men. These sites have special qualities.
After the creation, wearied from all their activity, the mythical creatures sank back into the earth and returned to their state of sleep. Sometimes their spirits turned into rocks or trees or a part of the landscape. The Aboriginal world is soul-permeated: groups may be linked to other groups through the travels of the Spiritual Beings; some of them may have given birth to living groups of people who either are associated with other groups that the Beings once visited on their travels or who have a common pedigree and may be defined through (patrilineal) descent from the same father; ghosts of the dead may still haunt the forests and evil spirits may inhabit rocky mountains. It is these mythic beings that are credited with having established social order and its 'laws'.
The Aboriginals believe that their ancestors were taught about their tribal lands by the mythical Beings, and were told how they, as descendants of these Beings, should behave. Their teachings are as important to them as the Ten Commandments were to the ancient Hebrews. The Dreamtime continues in the spiritual lives of Aboriginal people today. The events of the ancient era of creation are enacted in ceremonies and danced in mime form. Songs are chanted incessantly to the accompaniment of the didgeridoo or clap sticks. They relate the story of events of those early times and bring the power of dreaming to bear on life today. To Indigenous people land is not just something that they can own or trade. Land has a spiritual value. Whenever a traditional Aboriginal person looks at the landscape, he or she always sees much more than just the physical features. There is a deep awareness of the presence of the Dreaming ancestors. All around are signs of their presence, their tracks, places where they had dug out valleys, split rocks or disturbed the ground in their passing. Sometimes too, their bodies or those of their enemies are perceived in rocks, boulders and trees. Their actual spirits are also there, not dangerous or unfriendly, living on in the world they made. It is possible to communicate with ancestor spirits. The bond that this creates is one of enormous strength. Overall, the earth is a 'mother' in a real sense.

Important key-concepts are

"'We don't own the land, the land owns us."

"The land is my mother, my mother is the land."

"'Land is the starting point where it all began. It is like picking up a piece of dirt and saying this is where I started and this is where I will go."

"'The land is our food, our culture, our spirit and identity."

"We don't have boundaries like fences, as farmers do. We have spiritual connections."

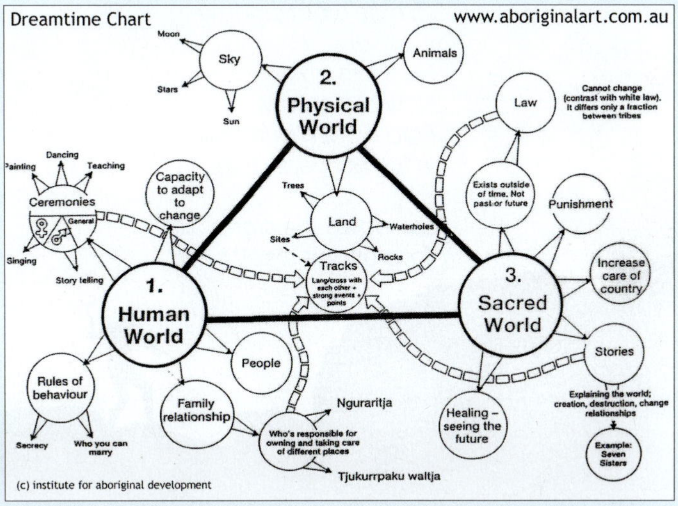

6

Oodgeroo Noonuccal

No More Boomerang

Oodgeroo Noonuccal (1920–1993) was the first of the modern Aboriginal protest writers. She was known for most of her life as Kath Walker, but then returned to the tribal name in 1988 in opposition to the Bicentenary celebrations of the conquest of Australia that appeared to be pure hypocrisy for her who had to work, at the age of 13, in domestic service and who was rejected as a nurse because of her Aboriginal origin. She became involved in the Aboriginal activist movement, seeking to generate cultural self-pride. – John Leonard, *Contemporary Australian Poetry* (Knoxfield: Houghton Mifflin Australia Pty Ltd., 1990), pp. 35f.

No more boomerang
No more spear;
Now all civilized –
colour bar and beer.

No more corroboree,
Gay dance and din.
Now we got movies,
And pay to go in.

No more sharing
What the hunter brings.
Now we work for money,
Then pay it back for things.

Now we track bosses
To catch a few bob,
Now we go walkabout
On bus to the job.

One time naked,
Who never knew shame;
Now we put clothes on
To hide whatsaname.

No more gunya,
Now bungalow,
Paid by hire purchase
in twenty year or so.

Lay down the stone axe,
Take up the steel,
And work like a nigger
For a white man meal.

No more firesticks
That made the whites scoff.
Now all electric,
And no better off.

Bunyip he finish,
Now got instead
White fella Bunyip,
Call him Red.

Abstract picture now –
What they coming at?
Cripes, in our caves we
Did better than that.

Black hunted wallaby,
White hunt dollar;
White fella witch doctor
Wear dog collar.

No more message-stick;
Lubras and lads
Got television now,
Mostly ads.

Lay down the woomera,
Lay down the waddy.
Now we got atom bomb,
End everybody.

Vocabulary

4 colour bar (n.): social barrier separating peoples of different colour - **6 din** (n.): loud noise - **13 to track** (v.): to follow - **14 few bob** (n.): some money (originally: shillings) - **15 walkabout** (n.): an Aborigine's period of nomadic wandering - **29 firestick** (n.): smouldering stick used for carrying fire from camp to camp - **30 to scoff** (v.): to mock - **39 cripes** (n.): interjection, colloquial (an expression of amazement, disgust, or the like), euphemistic for: "Christ!" - **41 wallaby** (n.): animal with large hind feet and a long tail, smaller than a kangaroo - **43 witch doctor** (n.): person who possesses magical powers - **44 dog collar** (n.): here: a stiff collar, worn by members of the clergy

Explanations

Intro: Bicentenary celebrations: the Bicentenary celebrations were held in 1988 in order to commemorate the 200th anniversary of European settlement in Australia. They mark the events of 26 January 1788, when the eleven ships of Captain Arthur Phillip's First Fleet arrived from Britain and gathered in Port Jackson to found the colony of New South Wales. - **Intro: Aboriginal activist movement**: movement for the advancement of Aboriginal rights - **5 corroboree** (n.): here: Aboriginal assembly of festive, sacred or warlike character - **21 gunya** (n.): Aboriginal hut - **33 bunyip** (n.): an imaginary creature of Aboriginal legend, said to haunt swamps and billabongs; cf. also: bunyip aristocracy: (*derogatory*) Australians who consider themselves to be aristocrats - **45 message-stick** (n.): a stick of about 10–30 cm, used by Aborigines to convey messages, also a kind of permit for s.b. passing through alien territory - **46 lubra** (n.): young Aboriginal woman - **49 woomera** (n.): a throwing stick, spear thrower, used to propel a spear - **50 waddy** (n.): Aboriginal heavy wooden war-club

Awareness

1 In class: Read the poem silently. Choose one stanza which you learn by heart. Recite the poem from memory together with twelve other students, each speaking one stanza aloud.

Comprehension

2 Give a rough idea of what you think the poem is about.
3 Write down in your own words what each stanza says. In class the task may be divided up and each student may choose the stanza he has learned by heart.

Analysis

4 Explain the basic principle according to which the poem is structured.
5 Make a list contrasting the aspects of Aboriginal life with those of civilisation.
6 Stanza five may be seen to be of central importance. Explain its meaning in the context of our Christian culture (cf. Genesis 1).
7 Examine the use of syntax, grammar, choice of words and explain the effect it is supposed to have on the reader.
8 Consider the improvements technological and economic progress has brought to the Aborigines and explain what the speaker wants us to realise.

Opinion

9 Do you think that the poem was a success? Give reasons for your view.
10 Is there anything which our western civilisation could learn from Aboriginal culture? Give reasons for your opinion.

Project

11 Try to turn this poem into a rap song.
Find a suitable rhythm to accompany the reading.
The students may form different groups and take turns reading the stanzas. They may also choose one speaker/singer who speaks/sings the first part of each stanza or each line and the "chorus" shouts the rest. Present the "song" to an audience.

Info

Aboriginal weapons

Throwing spears with woomeras

The weapons of Australia's Aborigines are well adapted to their nomadic life, in which ease of transport is a primary consideration. One important example is the boomerang, both the returning and the non-returning type. The former has come to symbolise traditional Aboriginal life but is mainly used for recreational purposes. The latter is used for hunting kangaroos, wallabies, birds, reptiles and fish and can cause serious injuries in warfare and duels. Hunting boomerangs can be up to two metres long and they are thrown at animals such as kangaroos or emus to break their legs or necks.

Other weapons that Aboriginal people have used since the Dreamtime are spears (up to six metres in length), stone knives, shields, clubs and fighting sticks. There are more weapons but these are the main ones used for hunting and fighting. Two of these instruments are mentioned in the poem: woomera and waddy.

The woomera is a spear-throwing device. It is actually a lever to increase the speed at which the spear travels. With the help of a woomera the spear can be thrown at a distance of 90 metres.

A waddy, also called nulla nulla, is a club made of wood used for hunting, fighting and digging.

7 "Crime Wave and Penal System in the 18th Century" *

The Australian governor Phillip (1788–1792) founded a system of labour in which people, whatever their crime, were employed according to their skills – as brickmakers, carpenters, nurses, servants, cattlemen, shepherds and farmers. From 1810 onwards, convicts were seen as a source of labour to advance and develop the British colony. Convict labour was used to develop the public facilities of the colonies – roads, causeways, bridges, courthouses and hospitals. Convicts also worked for free settlers and small land holders. Most of the convicts were thieves who had been convicted in the great cities of England. Only those sentenced in Ireland were likely to have been convicted of rural crimes. Transportation was an integral part of the English and Irish systems of punishment. Simple larceny, or robbery, could mean transportation for seven years. Compound larceny – stealing goods worth more than a shilling (about $50 in today's money) – meant death by hanging. – *Curiosities of Street Literature*, London, Reeves and Turner, 196, Strand, 1871. http://www.londonancestor.com/street/str-173.htm.

On John Austin: "Account of the Trial and Execution of JOHN AUSTIN. Convicted at the OLD BAILEY on Saturday, Nov. 1st, 1783, of a Cruel Highway Robbery on JOHN SPICER, a Poor Man. This robbery was so peculiarly inhuman and aggravated [...] John Spicer, the prosecutor, of Cray, in Kent, a poor labouring man, was coming to town on the Tuesday before, with his bundle, where he was a total stranger, in order to get into work, and met with the prisoner at Ilford, where they joined company, and travelled to town together. The prisoner, during their travelling together, sifted the prosecutor, and got out of him the nature of his journey, and what little property he was possessed of, undertook to get him a lodging, provide him a master, and to show him about London. After eating, drinking, and sleeping together on the road at different places, they arrived in town on the Thursday, when the prisoner took Spicer to a public house in Whitechapel, and left him there, pretending to go out after a lodging. Under this specious shew of friendship, Spicer was left for three or four hours, when a man whose name is Patrick Bowman (who also stands indicted, but is not yet taken) came to Spicer with a plausible apology for Austin's leaving him so long, and desired Spicer to go with him to Austin, who had got him a lodging. This the credulous prosecutor assented to, and Bowman took him to another public-house, where they joined Austin, and from thence they all went out, as Spicer thought, towards the lodging; but when he found himself in the middle of a field, out of the high road, by the side of a ditch, no house near, nor anything to be seen but the lights of some distant lamps, he observed that it was a very comical place to look after a lodging; upon which Austin retired a little, and Patrick Bowman drew a cutlass, with which he kept chopping at the hands, wrists, arms, body, and head of the prosecutor, and mangled him in a most shocking manner. [...] Austin being asked the usual question of what he had to say why judgement of death should not be pronounced against him, replied, "I don't fear death, as I am not guilty, and shall die innocent." The Recorder then addressed the prisoner as follows: "John Austin, you have been tried and convicted by a just and yet merciful jury, upon the most clear and satisfactory evidence. So horrid a crime as you have been guilty of, in its nature so audacious and inhuman, calls aloud for the very severe and immediate interposition of justice. It has been the declared intention of our merciful Sovereign, that he will never shew any compassion to such wretches as you, who add cruelty to robbery, and whose attacks on the property of his peaceable and honest subjects are accompanied with acts, whereby the crime of murder may he added to that of robbery. Everybody must applaud a resolution founded on the strictest justice and necessity. It is peculiarly my duty to further his royal intentions, by making my report of such criminals as you the first opportunity after conviction; and, therefore, to carry his Majesty's purpose into effect, I shall report you as a fit object of punishment with all possible speed. Your crime has been accompanied with every species of aggravation. Under the mask of friendship you have robbed a poor innocent man, deluded by your treacherous designs, and your false friendship: it is further aggravated by the baseness and inhumanity of your deceit, which cannot entitle you to any instance of mercy, but requires that you may be made an example of immediate justice. On Monday, therefore, I shall make the report of you to his Majesty. I advise you to prepare your soul for that fate which I am now about to pronounce against you." The Recorder then pronounced the usual sentence, and the prisoner was taken from the bar. THE EXECUTION. Yesterday morning was executed, at Tyburn, John Austin, convicted last Saturday of robbing John Spicer in a field adjoining the highway at Bethnal green, and cutting and wounding him in a cruel manner. From Newgate to Tyburn the convict behaved with great composure. While the halter was tying the unhappy wretch trembled in a very extraordinary manner, his whole frame appearing to be violently convulsed. The Ordinary having retired from the cart, the convict addressed himself to the surrounding populace in the following words, "Good people, I request your prayers for the salvation of my departing soul; let my example teach you to shun the bad ways I have followed; keep good company, and mind the word of God." The cap being drawn over his face, he raised his hands, and cried, "Lord have mercy on me, Jesus look down with pity on me, Christ have mercy on my poor soul;" and while uttering these exclamations, the cart was driven away. The noose of the halter having slipped to the back part of his neck, it was full ten minutes before he was dead."

Preparing the gallows for an execution

Vocabulary

6 prosecutor: (here) a claimant, in this case: the victim who raises a claim - **20 shew**: old for "show" - **34 cutlass** (n.): a short sword with a curved blade, used by sailors or pirates in the past - **36 to mangle** (v.): to injure - **40 recorder** (n.): here: a clerk who records, writes or copies documents - **48 interposition** (n.): intervention - **50 Sovereign** (n.): the supreme lawmaking authority, i.e. a monarch - **65 to delude** (v.): to deceive - **80 halter** (n.): here: the person who was in charge of putting the rope round the accused's head - **83 the Ordinary** (n.): an ecclesiastic, esp. a bishop, holding an office to which certain jurisdictional powers are attached

Explanations

2 Old Bailey: London's central Criminal Court; it is located 200 yards northwest of St Paul's Cathedral, just outside the former western wall of the City of London. The initial location of the courthouse close to Newgate Prison allowed prisoners to be conveniently brought to the courtroom for their trials - **6 Cray** (n.): a parish in Kent - **6 Kent**: a county in southeast England, located between London and the continent - **9 Ilford**: a small village in the county in the East of England - **18 Whitechapel**: a district in London - **75 Tyburn**: a village in the county of Middlesex, mostly known for the gallows (the "Tyburn Tree", i.e. a wooden triangle supported by three legs) standing in the middle of a roadway leading to London - **77 Bethnal**: an area east of London - **79 Newgate**: name of London's chief prison, built in 1188, at the corner of Newgate Street and Old Bailey, inside the city of London

Awareness

1 What do you know about corporal punishment predating the 18th century?

Comprehension

2 Write a bill of indictment for the above case.

Opinion

3 What makes the crime described in this report especially appalling?

Projects

4 As told in the story of William Thornhill (see pp. 7 ff.), some criminals in 18th and 19th century England escaped the gallows by being sent to the penalty colonies in Australia or New Zealand. What conditions awaited the prisoners transported to Australia? Also find pictures and photos (see e.g. http://images.statelibrary.tas.gov.au/ Search/Search.asp?Letter=L&Creator=Lempriere%2C+Thomas%2C+1796-1852).

5 Work about the life of the convict and artist Thomas Watling and on Augustus Earle.

6 Research on the present status of corporal punishment in different countries (see e.g. http://www.zona-pellucida.com/wilson02.html; http://www.corpun.com/ukju9803.htm), focussing on the question if corporal punishment is a useful deterrent (e.g. http://www.corpun.com/uksc9610.htm#panics).

8

John Rickard

"The European Settlers" *

By the late 19th century the convicts, too, had come to be regarded as pioneers whose struggle with the elements of a hostile world helped to shape the Australian nation. Together with other immigrants they settled the land, worked on farms, raised sheep and explored new land. The following text sheds a critical light on the effects of this European settlement on the environment and its native inhabitants. - John Rickard, *Australia - A Cultural History* (London: Longman, 1988), pp. 64ff.

Some settlers were worried about the effect of sheep and cattle on natural herbage, but of more dramatic concern was the wholesale destruction of forests. The often indiscriminate clearing of land became an Australian hallmark, and the skeletal remains of ring barked trees an eerie reminder of the European assault. Mining was also notorious for its appetite for timber, and its mushroom communities often existed in a landscape ruthlessly denuded of trees. But by the 1860s, influenced by the American G. P. Marsh's seminal *Man and Nature*, concern was being expressed at the loss of forest resources and the possible effect on climate. The early assumptions about improvements were giving way to a more critical assessment of the European impact on the environment.

It is possible that this new element of doubt – the sense in which the environment could be seen as taking its revenge on its exploiters – contributed to the myth of the alien land which had taken formal shape by the end of the century. The experience of the explorers in the interior, and the resistance of Aborigines to European settlement, were certainly factors. It is significant, too, that the 1890s, during which most of the literary basis to the myth was established, particularly through the agency of the popular weekly, the *Bulletin*, was a time of depression and drought, when the early Arcadian promise had turned sour.

From one perspective the function of the myth was to idealise the men and women who confronted the environment. Here the myth has taken different forms.

One version, dubbed the Australian legend, stresses the role of the shearers, the migratory workforce of the Outback. The peculiar labour needs of pastoralism helped create a kind of inter-colonial bush proletariat, recruited largely from the convicts or their sons, the 'Currency Lads'. Convict attitudes such as anti-authoritarianism and the 'freemasonry of felonry' were transformed by environment, it is argued, into a set of values democratic and collectivist which are personified in the noble bushman, 'the national culture-hero'. Another version celebrates the pioneers, usually identified as the settlers, whether pastoralist or farmer. Whereas the Australian legend gives the environment a purifying role, the pioneer variant casts settler and environment as adversaries. Assailed by flood, fire, drought and blacks, the settlers eventually 'won' the land. The pioneer tradition could also incorporate women, while the shearer-derived legend was specifically male. Indeed as civilisers of the wilderness women could be accorded a special recognition: as one poet put it, 'The hearts that made the Nation were the Women of the West'."

It was understandable that such legend making should usually present the environment in its starkest form, the outback or Never-Never. But this was not necessarily the landscape which principally concerned writers and artists, particularly in the early years of settlement. Yet whatever the scenery they described or painted, the wielders of pen and brush had to devise, or at least select, modes for perceiving the strange environment. Antipodal inversion was one such device, which helped create an emblematic language for the colonial writer. It sometimes led, quite naturally, to characterising the Bush in terms of 'weird melancholy'. The classic exposition was given by the novelist Marcus Clarke in 1874:

"In Australia alone is to be found the Grotesque, the Weird, the strange scribblings of Nature learning how to write. Some see beauty in our trees without shade, our flowers without perfume, our birds who cannot fly, and our beasts who have not yet learned to walk on all fours. But the dweller in the wilderness acknowledges the subtle charm of this fantastic land of monstrosities. He becomes familiar with the beauty of loneliness. [...] The phantasmagoria of that wild dreamland called the Bush interprets itself, and he begins to understand why free Esau loved his heritage of desert-sand better than all the bountiful richness of Egypt."

Convicts at work, Port Arthur, 1836

Vocabulary

2 herbage (n.): vegetation, grass - **5 hallmark** (n.): feature - **6 eerie** (adj.): mysterious - **9 to denude** (v.): to make naked or bare - **10 seminal** (adj.): creative, having an influence on the future - **26 Arcadian** (adj.): pastoral, idyllic - **31 to dub** (v.): to nickname - **32 migratory** (adj.): characterised by wandering - **37 felonry** (n.): felony - **62 wielder** (n.): s.o. who has power - **79 phantasmagoria** (n.): illusion - **82 bountiful** (adj.): mild, generous, characterised by good quality and excellence

Explanations

10 G. P. Marsh: George Perkins Marsh (1801-1882) was not only an American diplomatist and United States minister, but also a scholar of great wisdom whose subjects ranged from philology, the study of reptiles, engravings, comparative grammar or music to physiognomy and geography. He published works like *The Camel, His Organization, Habits and Uses* (1856), *Lectures on the English Language* (1860) and *Man and Nature* (1864) (revised as *The Earth As Modified by Human Action* in 1874) which made him the fountain-head of the conservation movement. - **21 Aborigines**: see p. 10 - **25 Bulletin**: a weekly which after its first issue in Sydney in Januar 1880 under the editorship of John Feltham Archibald (Jules François) and John Haynes became the rallying point for Australian nationalism and is sometimes seen as the Bushman's Bible. It is also known for discovering Australian poets and writers like e.g. Henry Lawson and A. B. Paterson. - **33 outback** (n.): the Australian interior - **36 Currency Lad** (n.): a term used in the early days of settlement in New South Wales to distinguish the Australian-born native youths from the British-born who were called Sterling - **37 freemasonry**: teachings of the worldwide secret society of freemasons that impels its members to live according to a certain system of values, often attracting freethinkers and political radicals - **57 Never-Never** (n.): a term applied since the 1880s to an area of undefined extent of the Northern Territory. The origin may have been a misunderstanding of an Aboriginal word ('nievah vahs') meaning unoccupied land. - **70 Marcus Clarke**: a novelist, journalist and miscellaneous writer (1846-1881) who inquired into the dominant note of Australian scenery and found it in the 'note of Poe's poetry' (Weird Melancholy), since he considered the Australian mountain forests to be funereal, secret and stern and saw their solitude as desolation. For him they were fear-inspiring and gloomy. If placed before the frightful grandeur of those barren hills, the soul, according to Marcus Clarke, would drink in their sentiments of defiant ferocity and would be steeped in bitterness. - **81 Esau**: the elder of the twin sons of Isaac and Rebecca, who sold his birthright to his brother Jacob and was tricked out of his father's blessing by his brother. He is seen as the traditional ancestor of the Edomites.

Awareness

1 What do you know about the early civilisation in your region?

Comprehension

2 Name the different ways of how the early settlers regarded their environment.

Analysis

3 What conditions contributed to the legend-making that developed into the Australian myth?

4 Make a list of words and expressions the author uses to denote the process of 'civilising' Australia. Comment on his values and judgements.

Opinion

5 Do you think that a society needs mythical patterns in order to stabilise its identity?.

Projects

6 What role did the popular weekly *Bulletin* play in the emergence of an Australian identity? Work on this question by consulting a historical book on Australia, e.g. M. Clark: *A Short History of Australia* (2nd ed. South Melbourne, 1981) or *The Ashton Scholastic History of Australia* (Sydney, 1988); H. M. Green: *A History of Australian Literature* (rev. by D. Green, 2 vols., London, 1984), L. Kramer (ed.), *The Oxford History of Australian Literature* (Melbourne/Oxford, 1981) or *The Cambridge Encylopedia of Australia* (Cambridge University Press, 1994).

7 Compare the myths that accompanied the colonisation of Australia and the USA.

9

Rolf Harris

"Tie Me Kangaroo Down, Sport"

The song "Tie Me Kangaroo Down, Sport" became very popular in the early 1960s. The composer and singer Rolf Harris created a special type of music by means of a "wobble board", a thin sheet of hardboard (wood) which, when flexed back and forth, makes a charming sound with which to keep to the beat. It is similar to a pendulum because the time of each swing of a pendulum depends on the length of the pendulum string. Harris decided the sound was just the background he needed for his kangaroo song. The song immediately rocketed to the top of the Australian bestseller list. Its appeal to some degree lies in its nonsensical lyrics, which can only be understood by Australians!

There are various versions of the lyrics. Here is one of them.

Spoken Introduction: "There's an old Australian stockman, lying, dying. He gets himself up on one elbow, turns to his mates, who are gathered round, and he says:

'Watch me wallaby's feed, mate, watch me wallaby's feed. They're a dangerous breed, mate, so watch me wallaby's feed.'

All together now! Tie me kangaroo down, sport, Tie me kangaroo down. Tie me kangaroo down, sport, Tie me kangaroo down.

Keep me cockatoo cool, Curl, Keep me cockatoo cool. Don't go acting the fool, Curl, Keep me cockatoo cool.

All together now! Tie me kangaroo down, sport …

Take me koala back, Jack, Take me koala back. He lives somewhere out on the track, Mac, So take me koala back.

All together now! Tie me kangaroo down, sport …

Mind me platypus duck, Bill, Mind me platypus duck. Don't let him go running amuck, Bill, Mind me platypus duck.

All together now! Tie me kangaroo down, sport …

Play your didgeridoo, Blue, Play your didgeridoo. Keep playing 'til I shoot thro', Blue, Play your didgeridoo.

All together now! Tie me kangaroo down, sport …

Part of a didgeridoo, the famous musical instrument of the Aborigines

Tan me hide when I'm dead, Fred, Tan me hide when I'm dead. So we tanned his hide when he died, Clyde …

(*spoken*) … And that's it hanging on the shed.

All together now! Tie me kangaroo down, sport, Tie me kangaroo down. Tie me kangaroo down, sport, Tie me kangaroo down.'

(The fourth verse of the original version was removed – it read: "Let me Abos go loose, Lou, Let me Abos go loose. They're of no further use, Lou, So let me Abos go loose.")

Australia's most famous animal: the kangaroo ...

... and the related, but smaller wallaby

Although a platypus has a beak, it is a mammal

Vocabulary

4 stockman (n.): a man whose job is to take care of farm animals - **10 sport** (n.): an Australian term of address, alluding to "good sport", which often, as in this case, praises s.o. for carrying out a small favour you are asking of them - **13 cockatoo** (n.): an Australian parrot with a lot of feathers on the top of its head - **18 koala** (n.): an Australian animal like a small grey bear with no tail that climbs trees and eats leaves - **22 platypus** (n.): a small furry Australian animal that has a beak and feet like a duck, lays eggs, and produces milk for its young

Explanations

5 gets up on one elbow: that would presumably be his right elbow, which is probably very strong, from years of holding up the bar at the local watering hole, also known as a pub (public house, hotel, tavern) - **5 he turns to his mates**: his mates are more stockmen, and loafers from the pub. He turns to look them in the eye, because eye contact is a sign of sincerity, and since he's dying, that's a fair dinkum (sincere) thing to do. - **7 wallaby** (n.): an Australian animal like a small kangaroo - **7 Watch me Wallaby's feed**: definitely poor grammar: It should be "watch my Wallaby's feed". - **7 feed** (n.): Wallabys commonly eat grass during the hours of darkness - **8 dangerous breed**: This is a joke. Wallabys are very quiet creatures, and make good household pets. - **13 Curl** (n.): abbreviation, short for Curley, which is a reference to curly hair - a nickname applied to men with straight hair, which is an unusual trait in the outback. - **26 didgeridoo** (n.): a long wooden musical instrument, played especially in Australia - **26 Blue** (n.): nickname for a man with red hair (to have a blue: to have a fight, which is supposed to be a common occurrence when dealing with Australian men having the phenotype of red hair) - **27 keep playing till I shoot thro, Blue**: The phrase to "shoot thro" is an abbreviation of "shoot through", which is Australian language for "leave" - **30 tan me hide**: the process of tanning hides, in this case referring to the skin of the leathery old stockman. Generally, the skin is removed, and sprinkled with salt to dry out the moisture. The hide is then wrapped with the bark of the turpentine tree and left to cure for 3 months. At that time, the hide is unrolled, and may be hung on the side of the shearing shed, where it is an object of veneration, or used as a particularly utilitarian door mat. Nothing is wasted on outback pastoral stations. - **30 Fred**: nickname for any man whose name is not Frederick - **37 Lou**: sometimes in other versions also Lew or Bruce (which is the name of Harris' brother) - **37 Abos** (n.): highly pejorative term for the Australian indigenous people, the aboriginals - **37 Let me Abos go loose, Lou**: suggests that the stockman had some Aborigines working for him, like servants or ranch hands who should be freed or, as another interpretation suggests, be fired

A stockman at work

Awareness

1 Which Australian celebrities do you know? Categorise them according to the types of their activities (arts, film, music, sports).

2 Which animals often associated with and typical of Australia do you know?

Comprehension

3 Enumerate all the elements that are indicative of what may be seen as ingredients of "Australianness".

4 Characterise a stockman's behaviour and occupation.

5 National symbols and stereotypes serve to affirm one's identity. What is associated with a stockman?

Analysis

6 Determine the tone of the song.
7 Find out the rhetorical devices that reinforce the humorous character of the song.

Opinion

8 Would you like living as a stockman? Justify your opinion.

Projects

9 Harris explained in an interview with Radio Scotland in 2006: "I was 27 or something when I wrote that. But since 1960, I have never sung that verse" (i. e. the fourth verse). Trace the history of the song, its different versions and the controversies it has aroused (e.g. http://www.theage.com.au/news/music; http://www.mudcat.org/thread.cfm?threadid=43491; http://australian-literature.suite101.com/article.cfm/book_review_tie_me_kangaroo_down_sport).
10 Work on other stereotypes that reinforce "Australian" values and contribute to "Australian-ness" (e.g. http://valuesaustralia.com).
11 Do some research into the "wobble board" and try to paint it (http://www.rolfharris.com).

The family entertainer **Rolf Harris** was born in 1930 in Bassendean, a suburb of Perth. He was educated at Perth Modern School in 1948, then went to Claremont teachers college from 1950 to 1951. He was a champion backstroke swimmer, a talented artist and performer and left Australia to become an arts student in England. He became a very popular entertainer on English television. During the 1950s and 1960s, he was very well known in Australia and England for songs such as "Tie me Kangaroo Down, Sport", which were to a certain degree inspired by Harry Belafonte's songs. All these songs appealed to families and children, but mostly they were popular because of their Australian idiosyncrasies.

10

Angus McIntyre

Ned Kelly – a Folk Hero? Three incidents from the life of the famous bushranger*

There were several kinds of bushrangers in Australian history. The last wave, the so-called wild colonial boys, were the sons of free poor settlers, who combined their contempt of authority with a spirit of adventure. Some of them were ruthless murderers, but others were admired for their courage and their skill with horses and weapons. They liked to show off and dressed and acted in a way supposed to provoke the authorities and the respectable people, a behaviour referred to as "flashness". They used to carry colt revolvers, knives and rifles and sometimes masked their faces with large coloured handkerchiefs. The most famous of these "wild boys" was Ned Kelly, who, in the eyes of many, has become Australia's foremost folk hero. Ned Kelly defied the law and the lawmen's bullets by wearing a home-made helmet and body armour made of iron which became part of his legend. Angus McIntyre describes three crucial events in the life of the most famous (and admired) Australian bushranger. – Angus McIntyre, "Ned Kelly, a Folk Hero", in: John Caroll, ed., *Intruders in the Bush. The Australian Quest for Identity* (Melbourne: OUP, 1982), pp. 38f., 41ff.

The Fitzpatrick Affair

On 15 April 1878, an incident occurred, which in the opinion of the 1881 Royal Commission of Enquiry into the Victorian Police, precipitated the outbreak of the Kelly Gang. This was the attempt by Constable Fitzpatrick to arrest Ned's younger brother, Dan, at his mother's hut at Eleven Mile Creek near Greta on a charge of horse stealing. A fracas ensued. Later that night, Fitzpatrick turned up in Benalla with what he claimed was a bullet wound in the wrist which, he said, had been inflicted on him by Ned Kelly. On the strength of this and related claims by Fitzpatrick, warrants were issued against Ned Kelly for shooting with intent to murder, and against Dan Kelly, Mrs Kelly, her neighbour, Williamson, and son-in-law, Skillion, for aiding and abetting this shooting.

When the police arrived to enforce these warrants, the Kelly brothers were nowhere to be found. They had to be content, therefore, with the arrest of Mrs Kelly, Skillion, and Williamson. One month later, on 17 May, Mrs Kelly was granted bail, Then, on 9 October, at the Beechworth Assizes, a jury found Mrs Kelly and the two men guilty of the abovementioned charges. On 14 October, the presiding judge, Sir Redmond Barry, sentenced her to three years jail and Skillion and Williamson to six years each.

The Cameron Letter

The day after the Euroa bank robbery, the wife of a station hand at Younghusband's, Mrs Fitzgerald, posted a letter which Ned Kelly had entrusted to her. It was addressed to Mr Cameron, MLA, and subsequently became known as the Cameron Letter. In it, Kelly criticized Whitty and Burns, two squatters, for mistreating the 'poor men of the district'. Also, he argued that the shooting of Lonigan, Scanlan, and Kennedy 'cannot be called wilful murder for I was compelled to shoot them in my own defence or lie down like a cur and die'. And he again made reference to Mrs Kelly having been sent to jail with a baby at the breast. This sentimental attitude towards his mother coloured his language. He claimed, for example, that his mother, his brother-in-law, Skillion, and his neighbour, Williamson, were as 'innocent as the child unborn' of having committed any offences against Fitzpatrick. Also, he described the police, whom he accused of terrorizing his younger brothers and sisters, as never having had 'any relation or a mother or must have forgot them'.

EDWARD (NED) KELLY

V. R.

£8000 REWARD

ROBBERY and MURDER.

WHEREAS EDWARD KELLY, DANIEL KELLY, STEPHEN HART and JOSEPH BYRNE have been declared OUTLAWS in the Colony of Victoria, and whereas warrants have been issued charging the aforesaid men with the WILFUL MURDER of MICHAEL SCANLON, Police Constable of the Colony of VICTORIA, and whereas the above-named offenders are STILL at LARGE, and have recently committed divers felonies in the Colony of NEW SOUTH WALES: Now, therefore, I, SIR HERCULES GEORGE ROBERT ROBINSON, the GOVERNOR, do, by this, my proclamation issued with the advice of the Executive Council, hereby notify that a REWARD of £4,000 will be paid, three-fourths by the Government of NEW SOUTH WALES, and one fourth by certain Banks trading in the Colony, for the apprehension of the above-named Four Offenders, or a reward of £1000 for the apprehension of any one of them; and that, in ADDITION to the above reward, a similar REWARD of £4000 has been offered by the Government of VICTORIA, and I further notify that the said REWARD will be equitably apportioned between any persons giving information which shall lead to the apprehension of the offenders and any members of the police force or other persons who may actually effect such apprehension or assist thereat.

(Signed) HENRY PARKES, Colonial Secretary, New South Wales.

(Signed) BRYAN O'LOGHLEN, Attorney General, Victoria.

Dated 15th February, 1879.

Ned concluded the letter with a monstrous threat. He wrote:

[...] but I wish to give timely warning that if my people do not get justice and those innocents released from prison and the Police wear their uniforms I shall be forced to seek revenge of everything of the human race for the future.

With no offence (remember your railroads) and a sweet goodbye

from
EDWARD KELLY
a forced outlaw

Glenrowan

[The Kelly gang ...] bailed up the inhabitants of Glenrowan and held them captive in Mrs Jones's hotel. [...] Not long after the first clash with the police, Ned Kelly left the hotel by the back and selected his horse, which he led away into the bush at the rear. On the way he apparently dropped his rifle and the skull cap which he wore inside his iron headpiece. He tried, it seems, to take off his armour but was unable to do so. Then he attempted to break through the police cordon in order to rejoin his comrades in the hotel.

What followed moved even the Royal Commissioners to eloquence:

"As the tall figure of the outlaw, encased in iron, appeared in the indistinct light of the dawn, the police for a time were somewhat disconcerted. To some it seemed like an apparition; others thought it was a black man who had donned a nail can for a joke, but as the shots from Martini Henry rifles, at short range, were found to have no effect, the sensation created seemed to have been akin to superstitious awe. One man described it as the 'devil', another as the 'bunyip'. Ned Kelly advanced until within a stone's throw of the hotel, when, in the vernacular of the bush, he defied the police, and called on the other members of the gang to come out of the hotel and assist him.'

Sergeant Steele finally brought Ned down with a shot which hit him beneath his armoured covering. He then rushed forward and grappled with him. Others ran to his assistance and, together, they removed Kelly's armour and carried him to the railway station.

Vocabulary

4 to precipitate (v.): to cause s.th. to happen sooner - **4 outbreak** (n.): a sudden occurrence (usually of s.th. unpleasant) - **15 to abet** (v.): to help s.b. to commit an offence - **20 bail** (n.): money left with a court of law to make sure that a prisoner will return when their trial starts - **28 station hand** (n.): worker on a sheep-station - **33 MLA**:

Member of the Legislative Assembly - **36 squatters** (n.): big landowners (cf. explanations) - **44 cur** (n.): (old fash.) an unfriendly dog, especially one that is a mix of several breeds - **70 to bail up** (v.): round up, gather - **77 skull cap**: cap worn inside a helmet to protect the head - **83 cordon** (n.): line or ring of police officers - **92 to disconcert** (v.): to confuse, upset - **95 to don** (v.): to put on - **98 akin to** (adj.): similar to - **100 bunyip** (n.): monster (*Austral.*) (cf. text 6, p. 20f.) - **101 vernacular** (n.): a form of a language that ordinary people use, especially one that is not the official language - **101 to defy** (v.): to refuse to obey or show respect for s.b.

Explanations

Intro: flashness or flashiness (n.): deriving from *flash*: a sudden short blaze of intense light; it also came to mean the "exaggerated display" of s.th., especially jewels, e.g. *a flash of diamonds.* The adjective **flashy** is normally used derogatively and refers to s.th. attracting attention by being large, bright or expensive but not of good quality or in good taste, e.g. *flashy clothes, a flashy car.* - **7 Eleven Mile Creek**: small river - **7 Greta**: small town in Victoria - **9 Benalla**: town in Victoria, north of Melbourne - **21 Beechworth Assizes**: lawcourt held in the town of Beechworth - **27 Euroa**: town in Victoria, north of Melbourne - **29 Younghusband's**: a sheep-station near Euroa - **36 squatters** and **selectors**: many Australians can trace roots back to transported convicts who, having served their sentences, stayed in Australia as free men, of a class known as selectors, because they were entitled to select a piece of land on which to live. Squatters on the other hand were not usually of convict descent but had come to Australia as free colonialists, taken up a choice piece of land and used convicts as their labour force. - **39 ff. Lonigan, Scanlan, Kennedy**: policemen who trailed the Kelly Gang - **86 Royal Commission of Enquiry**: commission, usually judicial, appointed by the British government to look (enquire) into and report on some aspect of public affairs - **96 Martini-Henry rifle**: a type of rifle which was used in the British Army

Awareness

1 Collect material on the life of Robin Hood. Find out why he was an outlaw and how he became a folk hero.

Comprehension

2 How did Ned Kelly become an outlaw?
3 What did Ned think of himself? How did he judge his situation? Refer to the Cameron letter. What happened to him in the end?

Analysis

4 Which people regarded Ned as a folk hero and which as an outlaw? Explain why he was regarded in such different ways.
5 Ned Kelly's enormous popularity shows that many Australians identify at least with part of his character. Explain which "typically Australian qualities" Ned stands for. You may refer to texts 11 (p. 32), 13 (p. 40), 16 (p. 47) and "Waltzing Matilda" (p. 5).

Opinion

6 How would you judge the behaviour of the police towards Ned and his relatives?
7 How far was Ned Kelly himself responsible for his situation?

Projects

8 Write an article for a local newspaper covering the trial of Ned Kelly.
9 Imagine you are a director and are going to make a film of the life of Ned Kelly. Write a script which shows how you would present these episodes on the screen. The script should include the dialogue and rough descriptions of the setting, lighting, camera work and action. Work in three groups, each covering one episode.

Vocabulary Info Box p. 32

5 dwelling (n.): place where people live - **7 daring** (n.): courage - **7 defiance** (n.): open refusal to obey s.b. or show respect for s.b. - **8 to roam** (v.): to walk or travel without any definite aim - **21 starvation** (n.): lack of food - **26 to raid** (v.): to make a sudden attack (and destroy)

Info

Bushrangers

The word "bushrangers" has changed over the years. In the early days of Australian history it referred to men who were good at hunting and riding and had the skills needed to survive in the Australian bush. Eventually it came to mean any criminal who lived in the bush and made his living out of plundering travellers and bush dwellings. It was often used synonymously with "bandits" or "robbers" who stole cattle and even murdered people. Today the word has adopted a more romantic meaning and is used with reference to men of daring who, in defiance of authority, were roaming the bush wild and free.

On the Australian gold fields

According to their motives we may distinguish between three different groups of bushrangers:

The *convict bushrangers* tried to escape from the hard life in the penal colonies of New South Wales and Van Diemen's Land. They had been brought to Australia as convicts in the late 18th and early 19th centuries and lived a mean life in crowded prisons with poor food, hard labour and brutal punishments. They had nothing to lose, harboured no respect for the rights of others and were greatly feared. But they also had little chance of surviving in the bush for long. Some died of starvation or sickness, others were killed by the police and landowners. Those who were captured alive were hanged or died in prison.

The *gold rush* of the 1850's and 1860's in New South Wales and Victoria brought about people who preferred stealing to working. They formed gangs and held diggers up on the lonely roads near the goldfields, raided wealthy properties near the gold towns or robbed the gold escorts to the cities.

The last wave of bushrangers were the so-called *wild colonial boys* (cf. introduction on p. 29).

11

John Rickard

"Sports and Mateship"

Australia has a climate which is ideally suited for outdoor activities, sports (e.g. cricket, soccer, bowls, golf, netball, tennis, basketball, field hockey, horse racing, yachting) and for outdoor living. Both these natural and the historical conditions of convictivism and of civilising an unknown continent, which made mutual support necessary, may account for the concept of mateship which is sometimes seen as the central Australian value or even as distinctively Australian. According to this ideal, the Australian "matey" man appears as a tough and independent comrade. The fact that mateship is an exclusively male phenomenon and often associated with values and practices such as manliness, drinking beer, larrikinism (a larrikin: originally: playboy, also: rowdy) and male chauvinism is, of course, highly provocative to the advocates of gender and human equality who focus on the hostility and violence of mates not only towards women, but also towards different racial or ethnic groups. - John Rickard, *Australia - A cultural history* (London/New York, 1986), pp. 98 ff., 177f.

Sports

A temperate climate was a natural inducement to outdoor sport activities, but it was the gathering pace of urbanisation which provided the incentive for the development of spectator sport. The gradual introduction of the Saturday half holiday was a response to the demand for leisure opportunities, but in turn helped create the demand for spectator sport. The early colonists had brought with them traditional British leisure pursuits. The British love of horses, for example, was easily accommodated in the colonial setting, even if it meant, as in the early years at Fremantle, racing horses along the beach; to this was added a colonial passion for gambling which derived at least in part from the fatalism of the convict temperament. But racing as a mass entertainment came later, an event of symbolic importance being the running of the first Melbourne Cup in 1861. A handicap race, it soon acquired a local and then, more surprisingly, a national popularity. By 1870 there was a crowd of 30,000 attending, and the day itself (at this time a Thursday, today the first Tuesday in November) was already becoming something of a bank holiday in Melbourne.

Australia's cricketers retain 'the Ashes' in England (2001)

Cricket, too, already had a history when the British made their settlement in 1788; indeed, in that very year the Marylebone Cricket Club had set out rules for the game. However as with other sports there was still much variation in the way the game was played, and codification awaited the development of regular and organised competitions. When the first English team came out in 1862 their tour was promoted by two colonial entrepreneurs; the visitors' eleven would usually play 22 colonists, judged an appropriate handicap. There was enormous public interest, even though the playing relationship between English and colonial resembled that between teacher and student. The first Australian tour of England was made by an Aboriginal team, but although the players were proficient it seemed to be sponsored more for its antipodean oddity. It was not until the 1880s that the rhythm of reciprocal tours was established, and the successful Australian team of 1882 returned from England with, for the first time, the 'Ashes' of English cricket. The relationship of friendly but intense imperial rivalry had been set.

Mateship

Disappointed men clung to a tradition of mateship, a domain of male values from which women were largely excluded. Whether or not mateship was born as a response to the pioneering hardships in the bush, as is the conventional wisdom, it soon became a part of the colonial culture, as much at home, say, in the folklore of trade unionism as in rural mythology. Anzac took over the values of mateship, giving them a patriotic dimension and, incidentally, reinforcing the male exclusiveness of the tradition.

Mateship, at one level, was a form of male sociability, an escape from the domestic environment. Pubs were basically a male preserve, and according to one social historian, for many workers 'the time in the pub at the end of each day was all that made life bearable, life without beer was unimaginable'. This drinking routine could be 'as fundamental to survival as food and sleep; it was more cathartic than sex'. The custom of 'shouting' – no drinker could leave a group before having 'shouted' a round of drinks – was an established ritual. Sport was in large measure an extension of this male world, because although women were permitted to watch and, in restricted forms, participate, the overriding ethos was masculine. The race-track, cricket ground and boxing stadium were venues where men could feel entirely at home – even if accompanied by women.

At another level mateship was an intense, personal experience, a one-to-one relationship. In colonial society, with its relative absence of women, the homosexual overtones of mateship (even the very word 'mate' carrying its sexual innuendo) have been remarked upon.

"The horses are off!" ... for the famous Melbourne Cup

Vocabulary

2 inducement (n.): s.th. that brings about and makes you do s.th. - **3 to gather** (v.): to develop - **20 handicap** (n.): a disadvantage imposed on a competitor to make the chances of success more nearly equal for all - **50 proficient** (adj.): experienced - **51 antipodean** (adj.): situated at or belonging to the opposite side of the earth, especially the region opposite our own - **56 Ashes** (n.): the name given to the competition between the English and Australian cricket teams; here: the victory in this competition - **78 preserve** (n.): a privileged area - **87 cathartic** (adj.): purifying - **91 to shout a round of drinks** (v.): to spend drinks - **97 overriding** (adj.): dominant - **99 venue** (n.): a place fixed for a contest or a match - **105 innuendo** (n.): a remark that suggests something sexual or unpleasant without saying it directly, or these remarks in general

Explanations

12 Fremantle: harbour of Perth in Western Australia - **19 Melbourne Cup**: the most famous horse race in Australia which was held for the first time in 1861, drawing e.g. in the 1880s more than 100,000 people and still doing so today. On Melbourne Cup day, public life in Victoria comes to a standstill. - **34 Marylebone**: in previous times a district of London, now part of the Greater London Borough Westminister, known e.g. for Regent's Park and zoological gardens - **69 Anzac**: the abbreviation for Australian and New Zealand Army Corps, founded in 1915, then becoming a general term for all Australian or New Zealand soldiers who are said to have been unbelievably brave and heroic fighters and have thus become icons in the Australian mind.

Awareness

1 Which of the photos in your book show that Australia is ideally suited for outdoor activities and sports?
2 Make notes on where and how you have become aware of Australia's sporting character.

Comprehension

3 How did the British way of life and culture influence Australia's obsession with sports?
4 Describe in your own words what, for a long time, the relationship between Australia and Britain was like.
5 How far can a cathartic effect be attributed to the "drinking routine" (l. 85) associated with mateship?
6 Enumerate the factors that have contributed to Australia's love of sport.

Analysis

7 Divide the paragraphs "A temperate climate ... had been set" (ll. 2–59) into their constituent parts and closely analyse how the author arranges his material.
8 The text mainly deals with the development of traditional British sports in19th century Australia. Henry Lawson, the most famous Australian writer of this era called it "a land where sport is sacred." This is also true of the 20th century. Only few people know that Australia is the only country in the world never to miss the Summer Olympics since 1896. Examine the figures given in the table on p. 35 and compare Australia's performance with that of Germany. A correct interpretation requires you to work out the per capita medal score.

Opinion

9. Why do you think some women are opposed to the concept of mateship?
10 Do you think that the basic concepts referred to in the text on mateship should be overturned or that they should rather be preserved as the last refuge for people who want to escape from a world overburdened with political correctness and monitored by self-appointed watchdogs?

Projects

11 Do some internet research on sports in Australia. Find out which kinds of sports are popular, describe them and show how Australia is doing internationally. Develop statistics to support your presentation.
12 Australia like every country in the world needs a view of history that creates and shapes her identity. Collect data and dates that in your view make up the kind of an ideal Australian identity that would make you like to emigrate to Australia.
13 The table on p. 35 shows the Olympic Summer Games medal tally for Australia and Germany. Find out how the United States, Great Britain and Russia performed in these years. Calculate the per capita medal score and compare it to that of Australia. Illustrate your figures with the help of graphs.

Olympic Summer Games
Medal Tally for Australia and Germany

City	Seoul		Barcelona		Atlanta		Sydney		Athens		Bejing	
Year	**1988**		**1992**		**1996**		**2000**		**2004**		**2008**	
Country	**AUS**	**GER**	**AUS**	**GER**	**AUS**	**GER**	**AUS**	**GER**	**AUS**	**GER**	**AUS**	**GER**
Gold	3	48	7	33	9	20	16	14	17	14	14	16
Silver	6	49	9	21	9	18	25	17	6	16	15	10
Bronze	5	45	11	28	23	27	17	26	16	18	17	15
Total	14	142	27	82	41	65	58	57	39	48	46	41

Info

Australian English – some examples

mate: a working partner; a companion; a fellow participant in some corporate activity (always a man). As a mode of address it indicates equality and friendliness.
Matilda: a swag (see below)
swag: clothes and possessions that someone who is travelling on foot carries wrapped in a cloth
waltzing Matilda: carrying the swag, an expression given currency by A. B. Paterson's poem with this title, composed in 1895 and published in *Saltbush Bill* J. P. (1917), since then achieving the status of an unofficial national anthem (cf. Waltzing Matilda, p. 5)

banana bender: a person from Queensland
billy: tea kettle
boozer: pub
butcher: small glass of beer
chunder: vomit
coldie: a beer
damper: bread made from flour and water
dinkum, fair dinkum: true, real, genuine ("I'm a dinkum Aussie"; "is he fair dinkum?")
G'Day: hello!
larrikin: a bloke who is always enjoying himself
jumbuck: sheep
Never-Never: the Outback, centre of Australia
No worries!: You're welcome!; No problem!; No big deal!
schooner: large beer glass in Queensland; medium beer glass in South Australia
sheila: a woman
strine: Australian slang and pronunciation
tucker: food

The Devil's Marbles in Northern Australia are as special as the country's language

12

Beverley Paine

"Homeschooling"

Homeschooling (also: homeschool; home education or home learning) is the education of children at home, typically by parents but sometimes by tutors, rather than in other formal settings of public or private school. Homeschooling is a educational alternative which appears popular in certain countries, especially the United States, and which seems to be gaining increasing popularity in Australia. Home education is a legal alternative to school education in Australia. State and territory governments are responsible for regulating home education and have different registration requirements; homeschooling families, however, are able, and encouraged, to develop curricula and learning programs to suit the educational and developmental needs of their individual children. Many Australian families choose to educate their children at home. Homeschooling is both rewarding and enjoyable. The Australian census does not track homeschooling families, but it was estimated that in 1995 some 200,000 families homeschooled in Australia. The authors of the text, Beverley Paine and her husband Robin, belong to the Australian experts on homeschooling. Their children are now adults. The eldest went to school part time and full time, but was mostly homeschooled and their youngest was totally unschooled. Beverly is the 'publication officer' of the Home Education Association. In addition, she manages some homeschooling oriented Yahoo groups. – http://homeschoolaustralia.com.

"Robin and I were classed as 'bright students' at school, who 'should do well'. Despite our brilliant start, he failed university and I failed Matriculation! This usually surprises people – most assume we're tertiary educated. ... Anyone can teach their children. Everyone has something of value that they can teach anyone. But homeschooling isn't just about teaching. It's about learning. And that was the first lesson our very young teachers – our children – taught us, way back in 1986. ... When our youngest was in his late teens I rather belatedly discovered the Charlotte Mason approach to education, and more recently think that Enki seems to blend the best of the Steiner and Montessori approaches. I'm envious of new homeschoolers – there is so much experience to draw on and so many curriculum resources available specifically written for homeschoolers. It would be so cool to be starting out now! At the seminar we're going to talk about what we'd do differently knowing what we do now. It's a tough topic and in our usual style we're brutally honest about our journey. We're not an ideal family, we're a real family. We can't go back. We live with the consequences of our actions. Our children live with the consequences of our actions. How does it all turn out? Is it what we wanted or expected? For some families homeschooling is over once their children become adults. I'm still asking questions about the educational process. Some people may know of me as a natural learning advocate. It's an interesting concept and I've got lots of ideas about learning naturally. I like to think I have evolved a different definition of natural learning, one that puts the parent in the centre of focus along with the child. I'm no 'delight-driven' 'child-centred' natural learning proponent! But I am a fan of John Holt's writing on the subject of education, and you'll find that blended with my particular brand of conservative parenting style. We'd like to spend some time talking about the role of fathers in home educating families. For more than a decade we thought that Robin's role was peripheral to our home education experience. Even now Robin isn't convinced that he had much to do with the education of his children, despite the very real evidence! I think that we tend to undervalue the people resources around us as we clamour to access bigger and better material resources. Once upon a time education was very people focussed: we learned through talking and doing together: through first-hand, hands-on, primary experiences. Little children still learn like that. Big children can too. So can adults. Homeschooling takes us back to real, effective learning. I wrote before that we're a 'real' family. Homeschooling was easy: five of us living together under the one roof wasn't! When times got tough, as they often did, friends would urge us to take a break, put the children into school. My health let us down all the time. We lived frugally through necessity. We burned the candle at both ends. ... Twenty years is a long time to get something right, to make it work and work well. We'd like to share with you the things that worked well for us. The things that made homeschooling easy, such as how to create an environment where learning happens effortlessly, without anyone even realising learning is happening! We've got a lot to say about homeschooling and a lot of experiences to share. [...] Cheers Beverley (and Robin) Paine".

Vocabulary

3 matriculation (n.): the formal process of entering a university – **4 tertiary educated**: the educational level following the completion of a school providing a secondary education, such as a high school, secondary school, or gymnasium, i.e. colleges, universities, and institutes of technology – **44 to clamour** (v.): to demand – **44 to access** (v.): to get access to – **55 frugal** (adj.): careful to buy only what is necessary – **56 to burn the candle at both ends**: to live at a hectic pace, to live a life that is lived frenetically and unsustainably by working or enjoying oneself late into the night only to begin again early the next day

Explanations

11 Charlotte Mason: a British educator (1842–1923). The Charlotte Mason method is centred around her principle: "Education is an Atmosphere, a Discipline, a Life." – **12 Enki**: a globally active eduational programme named after the Sumerian God of water, crafts, intelligence and creation. He was generally beneficent toward mankind and is portrayed in several myths as risking the other gods' disapproval by showing compassion for those treated unfairly. The organisation's identity can best be summarised by its motto "Education is not the filling of a pail, but the lighting of a fire" (W. B. Yeats). – **13 Steiner and Montessori**: Rudolf Steiner (1861–1925) and Maria Montessori (1870–1952) were the most innovative educators and theorists of education of the 20th century.

Awareness

1 Write a letter of complaint which revolves around what in your opinion might be wrong with German schools in general or with your school. You may refer to George Bernhard Shaw's provocative statement that parents "send their children to school; and there is, on the whole, nothing on earth intended for innocent people so horrible as a school. To begin with, it is a prison." (http://www.zona-pellucida.com/texts/shaw11.html)

2 Many religion-oriented parents prefer homeschooling. Why?

Comprehension

3 According to the text, what is the widespread prejudice against homeschooling parents?

4 Has the attitude towards homeschooling changed over the years? Find evidence from the text.

5 What, according to Paine, is undervalued in mainstream schools? What are her arguments in favour of homeschooling?

6 Do home educators take the easy option?

Analysis

7 By what stylistic means does Beverley Paine try to promote the case of homeschooling?

Opinion

8 Would you like to be homeschooled? Give reasons for your decision.

Projects

9 Investigate the educational approach and methodology of Charlotte Mason (see http://simplycharlottemason.com; http://www.infed.org/thinkers/et-mason.htm) and of John Holt (1923–1985) who is reputed to be the veteran homeschooler (see http://www.holtgws.com; http://www.thehomeschoolmagazine.com).

10 What should a school be like that follows the principles of Enki education (see http://www.enkieducation.org/html/homeschool-curriculum.htm)?

11 Write a profile on the "Melbourne Rudolf Steiner School" (http://www.mrss.com.au). Would you like to attend that school? Give reasons for your answer.

12 Prepare a classroom debate on the topic: "Homeschooling versus Stateschooling" (see http://www.time.com/time/magazine/article/0,9171,1181679,00.html).

13 Work on the legal and procedural regulations of homeschooling (see pp. 38f. and http://www.eduweb.vic.gov.au/edulibrary).

HOME SCHOOLING

Application for Registration for Home Schooling

The Education and Training Reform Regulations 2007 require that parents responsible for home schooling their child must register their child with the Victorian Registration and Qualifications Authority (VRQA) if their child is of compulsory school age. Ammendments to the *Education and Training Reform Act 2006*, which came into effect on 1 January 2010 changed the compulsory school age from 6–16 years to 6–17 years of age.

Registration to home school children beyond compulsory school age, that is over 17 years of age, is optional rather than compulsory. The VRQA can register a child who is 17 turning 18 during the year of home schooling. The VRQA cannot register a child who is 18 at the time of application.

An application to register a child must be made using the prescribed application form.

The VRQA will notify you in writing, within 14 days of receiving a completed application that complies with this registration, that your child has been registered for home schooling.

The date of registration for home schooling is determined by the VRQA and is generally the date the VRQA completes the processing of the application.

Privacy Statement

The collection of this information is required by the *Education Training and Reform Act 2006.*

Without this information we are unable to process your application for registration for home schooling. You are able to request access to the personal information that we hold about you, and request that it be corrected. Please contact the VRQA on 61 3 9637 2806.

INFORMATION FOR COMPLETING THE APPLICATION FORM

You must provide the name and address of each parent responsible for the home schooling of the child. A parent includes a guardian and any person who has parental responsibility for the child under the *Family Law Act 1975* (Cwlth) and any person with whom a child normally or regularly resides.

Any parent responsible for home schooling must disclose if there is any order of a court or a tribunal, or any enforceable agreement that prevents access to the child. Please ensure that you circle either 2(a) or 2(b).

The parent who will be responsible for the home schooling of the child must sign the application.

You must provide evidence of the child's birth date when you send in the form. Satisfactory evidence can include a copy of an original certificate, an extract of birth or a note from a doctor who can attest to the child's age.

There is no fee payable to the VRQA for this application. Details of students registered for home schooling will not be made public.

Further information is available in the *Support materials for the registration of home schooling in Victoria.* Please read this before completing this application form.

Please direct any queries to the Home Schooling Officer, VRQA on 61 3 9651 3293.

The application form, together with proof of age documentation, should be sent to:

Victorian Registration and Qualifications Authority
Home Schooling Officer
GPO Box 2317
Melbourne VIC 3001

Victorian **Registration & Qualifications** Authority

Level 6, 35 Spring Street
Melbourne VIC 3000

GPO Box 2317
Melbourne VIC 3001

T 61 3 **9637 2806**
F 61 3 9651 3266
vrqa@edumail.vic.gov.au

www.vrqa.vic.gov.au

APPLICATION FOR REGISTRATION OF CHILD FOR HOME SCHOOLING

1 *I/We *[insert full names of each parent responsible for home schooling of child]*

*Delete whichever is inapplicable.

of *[insert address below]*

Postcode

Telephone (optional)

Email (optional)

apply to register for home schooling. *[insert name and date of birth of any child to be home schooled]*

Name of child

Date of birth

Name of child

Date of birth

Name of child

Date of birth

Name of child

Date of birth

Name of child

Date of birth

2 Please circle the correct statement:

a) **No order of a court** or tribunal or enforceable agreement exists that prevents or restricts *me/either of us from access to my/our children named above that would prevent me/either of us from providing the home schooling.

b) **Yes, an order of a court** or tribunal or an enforceable agreement exists that affects the home schooling of the child to be home schooled. *(Attach details of that order or enforceable agreement.)*

3 *I/We undertake that *my/our children named in (1) above will receive regular and efficient instruction that:

a) taken as a whole, will substantially address the following learning areas:

- The arts
- English
- Health and physical education (including sport)
- Languages other than English
- Mathematics
- Science
- Studies of society and environment
- Technology

and

b) will be consistent with the principles underlying the Act, being the principles and practice of Australian democracy, including a commitment to:

- elected government
- the rule of law
- equal rights for all before the law
- freedom of religion
- freedom of speech and association
- the values of openness and tolerance.

Signed

Date

Notes

1 An enforceable agreement may include a child agreement or parenting plan under the *Family Law Act 1975* (Cwlth).

2 Under regulation 65(2)(c), an application for registration of a child for home schooling must be accompanied by evidence of the date of birth of the child.

3 Under section 4.9.3 of the *Education and Training Reform Act 2006,* it is an offence to wilfully make, or cause to be made, or provide, any false or misleading information in any matter relating to registration on the State Register under Chapter 4 of that Act. The maximum penalty is 10 penalty units.

Info

Websites directed by the Paines

- www.beverleypaine.com
- Beverley's Books http://www.beverleypaine.com
- Homeschool Australia http://homeschoolaustralia.com
- Australian Home Education Directory http://australian-home-education.com
- Australian Homeschool Curriculum http://australianhomeschoolcurriculum.com/
- Learning Naturally Group http://groups.yahoo.com/group/learningnaturally
- SA Home Ed Network http://sahome-ed.beverleypaine.com
- Unschool~Kidz! http://unschoolkidz.beverleypaine.com
- HomeschoolAustraliaFAQ http://groups.yahoo.com/group/HomeschoolAustraliaFAQ
- SA Chapter of the HEA http://groups.yahoo.com/group/SAChapterHEA
- Aussie Homeschool Campers http://groups.yahoo.com/group/aussiehomeschoolcampers
- Homeschool Australia Newsletter http://groups.yahoo.com/group/HomeschoolAustraliaNewsletter

13

Midnight Oil

Beds are Burning

On Sunday, 28 May 2000, more than 150,000 people walked across Sydney Harbour Bridge in an expression of support for reconciliation between indigenous people and the wider (mainly white) community of Australia. According to the *Sydney Morning Herald* (29 May 2000) the walk "put meaning back into the near exhausted public dialogue on a great unresolved question for all Australians, the relationship between black and white." The day before 1600 people had attended the Corroboree 2000 ceremony at the Sydney Opera House to celebrate national reconciliation. The white rock group Midnight Oil has always taken an interest in the Aborigines' struggle for their rights. Since the release of their first album in 1978 Midnight Oil have become one of the most famous, most political and probably most Australian of all Australian bands. Their catchy hit single *Beds Are Burning* (1987) even reached the US-American top charts and brought global attention to the problems of the Aborigines. It was played by the "Oils" in the closing ceremony of the Sydney Olympics. – The song was first released on the album *Diesel and Dust* (1987), Columbia Records (Sony Music), CDM 02-460005-10.

Out where the river broke
The bloodwood and the desert oak
Holden wrecks and boiling diesels
Steam in forty five degrees

The time has come
To say fair's fair
To pay the rent
To pay our share
The time has come
A fact's a fact
It belongs to them
Let's give it back

How can we dance when our earth is turning
How do we sleep when our beds are burning

Four wheels scare the cockatoos
From Kintore East to Yuendemu
The western desert lives and breathes
In forty five degrees

The time has come
A fact's a fact
It belongs to us all
Let's give it back

Holden wrecks somewhere in the outback

Vocabulary

2 bloodwood (n.): (*Brosimum Rubescens*) a eucalyptus tree that has reddish timber and yields a dark red gum – **2 desert oak** (n.): (*Allocasuarina decaisneana*) tree with feathery leaves found in the dry desert region around Central Australia, a young tree being tall and thin, an old tree full and bushy – **15 cockatoo** (n.): cf. explanations on p. 17

Explanations

3 Holden wreck (n.): broken down car; in 1948 Australia began to produce its own car, the Holden – **16 Kintore, Yuendemu**: settlements in the Northern Territory, Alice Springs area, in the desert. The highest temperature so far: 53 degrees Celsius

Awareness

1 Can you imagine what the problems between white Australians and Aborigines may be?

Comprehension

2 Consider ll. 1–4 and 15–18. Describe what the singer sees, feels and hears.

3 Who is the singer? What group of the Australian people does he belong to? Whom does he address?

Analysis

4 The speaker repeatedly says "The time has come" (ll. 5, 9, 19). What time does he mean? Explain what stylistic means he uses to illustrate his statements.

5 In what respect are the last four lines different from ll. 9–12?

6 Examine the central questions of the song and explain what they might imply.

Opinion

7 What is the attitude of the singer towards the problem addressed in the song? Would you share his opinion if you were a white Australian? Explain why you think so.

8 Why do you think the song was chosen to be performed at the closing ceremony of the 2000 Sydney Olympics?

Projects

9 Collect material on the origin and history of American Indians, Australian Aborigines and New Zealand Maori. Work in different groups. Each group gives an overview of the origin and history of one people so as to characterise its relationship with the white Anglo-Saxon fellow citizens. Illustrate the important points of your presentation with the help of pictures, videos, interviews, cartoons etc.

10 Write a letter of regret to an Aboriginal tribal chief in which you try to seek forgiveness for what the whites did to the Aborigines.

Midnight Oil – a band with a conscience

Having fronted the band for 25 years Peter Garret, lead singer of Midnight Oil, quit the group in December 2002 in order to concentrate fully on environmental activism. Until then Midnight Oil had probably shown more environmental and social awareness than any other rock group in the history of music. They had always been concerned with the problem of reconciliation and as the first white group started on a tour together with an Aboriginal group, the Warumpi band. After this famous Black Fella/White Fella tour of Indigenous communities they were asked by the Aborigines to write a song that would accompany the handover of Uluru (Ayers Rock) back to the Aboriginal people. The song they wrote, *The Dead Heart*, perfectly suited the occasion and helped to put the problem of Aboriginal land rights on the political agenda.

But it was not only Aboriginal problems that the band was concerned with. Their record *Blue Skye Mine*, e.g. was a song for asbestos miners in the Australian outback who had developed a range of cancers and respiratory diseases and frequently died at an early age. The same song was used to draw attention to one of the world's largest pollution incidents, the *Exxon Valdez* oil spill before the Alaskan coast. The Oils went to New York and, although forbidden to do so, played a gig outside *Exxon's* headquarters causing a traffic jam that brought areas of the city to a standstill.

After the split-up in 2002 the band only reunited once to perform at a concert on January 29, 2005, to raise funds for the tsunami victims. Lead singer Peter Garret joined the Australian Labor Party and in the 2004 General Elections won a seat in the House of Representatives. After the Labor Party won the elections in 2007 Garret became Minister for the Environmental Protection, Heritage and the Arts.

14 Immigration to Australia

Globalisation has set off a new migration wave; the opinion poll company Gallup did a survey from 2007 to 2009 in 135 countries to find out what people's intentions are. 16 percent of the world's population would like to, if possible, move permanently to another country. This trend has affected Australia: 25 million of the persons interviewed would like to move to the country "down under". People with and without refugee-like backgrounds come to Australia, e.g. in 1999 refugees from the Kosovo or from East Timor, but also many foreigners voluntarily like to settle down there. Thus, each year Australia's population increases as a result of net overseas migration: since 1998–99, net overseas migration has comprised 45% or more of population growth. Australia is an extremely popular destination for highly skilled young people wishing to start a new life in another country. The country's economy is strong and Australia is actively encouraging the immigration of skilled migrants (General Skilled Migration = GSM-program). Of course, the British are the largest immigrant group in Australia and Australia remains the most popular emigration destination for Brits. According to *manager magazin* (2006) (http://www.manager-magazin.de/magazin/artikel/ 0,2828,422774,00.html) the amount of Germans leaving their home country has never been higher, many of them settling down in either Australia or New Zealand. This trend coincides with Australia viewing herself as a 'nation of immigrants' that has, definitely since the early 20th century, supported immigration through various migration programmes, calling those who were not Australian citizens "Aliens" (http://www.immi.gov.au/media/publications/statistics/federation/timeline1.pdf).

What follows [on p. 43] is a listing by the country of birth for the Australian resident population (http://workpermit.com/news/2009-09-04/australia/british-are-the-largest-immigrant-group-in-australia.htm).

Immigration figures in 2005

More than 123,000 migrants settled in Australia in 2004–05, one of the highest intakes of the past 20 years and the biggest since the Howard government came to power. New Immigration Department figures show 123,424 people decided to call Australia home last financial year, the highest number since the 145,316 recorded in 1988–89. The 2004–05 intake was up by more than 11,000 on the previous year. Almost 45,000 people, or 36 per cent of the total, settled in New South Wales, and Victoria was the next most popular state with 30,581 migrants. [...] Immigration Minister Amanda Vanstone said the figures showed a steady rise in the migrant intake over the past decade, with arrivals increasing by 40 per cent since 1994–95. "Australia has a wonderfully rich and diverse society as a result, with nearly one in four of Australia's 20 million people born overseas," she said. "On top of these figures are the growing numbers of people becoming permanent residents after arriving in Australia, such as overseas students who apply for skilled migration onshore."

A total of 13,235 people arrived on humanitarian visas last year, 5,000 of them refugees – the highest number in a decade. Skilled migrants accounted for the biggest number – over 53,000 – more than double the figure recorded in 1994–95. The United Kingdom provided the biggest number of migrants in 2004–05, with 18,220 Britons settling in Australia. More than 25,000 people settled from Europe, including the UK, over 33,000 came from Asia and some 24,000 from Africa and the Middle East. About 21,000 people settled from the Oceania region, more than 17,000 of them from New Zealand. Some 2,000 North Americans also settled in Australia last year, and a similar number from South and Central America. (http://www.theage.com.au/news/NATIONAL/Immigration-numbers-over-123000/2005/12/31/1135915716249.html)

Country of Birth	Estimated Resident Population
United Kingdom	1,153,264
New Zealand	476,719
China	279,447
Italy	220,469
Vietnam	180,352
India	153,579
Philippines	135,619
Greece	125,849
Macedonia	120,649
South Africa	118,816
Germany	114,921
Malaysia	103,947
Netherlands	86,950
Lebanon	86,599
Sri Lanka	70,908
Serbia and Montenegro	68,879
Indonesia	67,952
United States	64,832
Poland	59,221
Fiji	58,815
Ireland	57,338
Croatia	56,540
Bosnia-Herzegovina	48,762

Vocabulary

7: intake (n.): reception, admission – **25 onshore** (adv.): located on the shore

A beautiful landscape in an attractive country: sunset at Broken Bay, Sydney

Explanations

8 Howard government: refers to John Howard who was Australian Prime Minister from 1996 to 2007 – **16 Amanda Vanstone**: a former Australian politician and the current Ambassador to Italy, taking office in June 2007. Under the Howard government, she was in charge of the Department of Immigration and Citizenship which became the centre of controversies because it implemented the Australian policies of mandatory detention of unauthorised arrivals. It was also accused of mistreating asylum seekers at Australian immigration detention facilities. – **26 humanitarian visas**: visas available for people who escape war, experience persecution or are subject to substantial discrimination in their homeland

Awareness

1 From which countries do people come that might get "humanitarian visas"? Refer to the chart.

Comprehension

2 Which groups of migrants try to find a residence in Australia?
3 What makes Australia an attractive immigration country?

Analysis

4 What makes the text appear objective and based on valid research?

Opinion

5 Do you support an immigration policy based on humanitarian grounds? Give reasons for your decision (see e.g.: http://www.numbersusa.com/PDFs/sortingthroughhumanitarianclashesinimmigration.pdf).

Projects

6 Make surveys on the rate of immigrants to Australia (see http://www.abs.gov.au/Ausstats).
7 Write a historical account on German immigrants to Australia (see http://museumvictoria.com.au or http://www.immi.gov.au/media/publications/statistics/federation/timeline1.pdf).
8 What experiences have Germans living in Australia had (see http://www.goethe.de/ins/au/lp/prj/far/aus/enindex.htm? Gain an insight into the application process by filling in the formula required from the "Australian Government Department of Immigration and Citizenship" (http://www.immi.gov.au/allforms/pdf/866.pdf).
9 Work on the measures implemented by Australia to cope with the problem of both legal and illegal asylum-seekers (http://www.ahrcentre.org/working_papers/2004_3_Asylum_Seekers.htm) and the criticism they aroused.
10 Australia puts a great emphasis on its values. Work on them as defined by the government (http://www.immi.gov.au/living-in-australia/values/background).
11 Download an "Australian Immigration Assessment Form" (http://workpermit.com/australia/appraisal_form.htm) and complete it (see also http://www.immi.gov.au/about/department/diac-plan/diac-strategic-plan-2009-12.pdf).

15

Alexander Chancellor

"The Queen is Dead ..."

"The crown and the Queen are not part of our dream!" was the republican motto for the referendum on the future of the monarchy held on November 6, 1999. Although the constitutional convention in Canberra recommended that Australia become a republic, monarchists and their allies won clear majorities in all but one of the six Australian states. About 55 per cent of Australians voted against the republican proposal so that the Queen remained head of state. In March 2000 she visited Australia for the first time after the referendum. - Alexander Chancellor, "The Queen is Dead, Long Live President Boonie," *The Guardian*, Saturday November 6, 1999.

Today, the Australians are not electing a president but voting on whether to get rid of the monarchy and proclaim a republic. Some 12 million of them will be going off to the polls, cans of Fosters in their hands, corks dangling from the brims of their hats, to take this momentous decision. But the turnout will be large only because voting is obligatory. Most Australians have displayed vast apathy during the referendum campaign. And although a majority of them support the principle of a republic, they may well reject it on this occasion because the proposed republican model would prevent them ever having somebody like Boonie as president.

They fear they would get a politician instead, and Australians, unlike the peoples of lesser nations, fear nothing more than a politician as head of state.

The idea of Australia having as head of state the queen of a country on the other side of the world strikes almost everybody as ridiculous. An opinion poll published in the Guardian this week revealed that even British people find it so, and feel that the Australians would do well to get rid of her. "What do Elizabeth II and the future Charles III mean to a Greek farmer's grandson bred in the Snowy Mountains, or to the Sydney-born daughter of a Lebanese engineer?" asks Robert Hughes, the distinguished Australian writer and art critic. "About as much as Prince Michael of Greece or the former King Zog of Albania do to me – the fourth-generation descendant of an immigrant Irish grocer."

Arrival of Queen Elizabeth II

But according to an excellent article in the Sydney Morning Herald this week, it is the very absurdity of the monarchy that gives it its value to Australians. Dr Peter Slezak, a lecturer in science and technology at the University of New South Wales, said that "the very anachronism of our British heritage, and a faintly ridiculous royalty, serves a vital social function which has been overlooked [...] the function of the monarchy for Australia is to help preclude the bearers of real power from revered, heroic status". Slezak applauded the Australians for their resistance to American-style nationalism and flag-waving sentimentality: "It is inconceivable that Australian children would recite allegiance to the flag, or that any politician could end a speech earnestly declaring 'God Bless Australia'."

"Australians recognise that the spirit of the nation is captured not in contrived nationalistic zeal, but in the jolly swagman's irreverence for symbols of authority and privilege," he went on. "Such a larrikin, critical attitude is at the heart of liberal democracies because it reflects dependent thought rather than slavish conformity." If Australians reject a republic today, it will be because they don't want a system under which the politicians would have the power to choose the president and would almost certainly not choose anyone like Boonie. It will also be because they don't want the prime minister to have the power to sack the president "with more ease than he could his driver or cook" (as the monarchist campaigner, Kerry Jones, has put it).

Whatever happens today will not be the end of the story. If the monarchists win, the campaign for a republic will be resumed before long. If the republicans win, a campaign will begin for a constitutional amendment to allow for a directly elected president. [...]

Vocabulary

4 to go to the polls (v.): to vote – **5 to dangle** (v.): to hang or swing loosely – **5 brim** (n.): here: the edge of a hat. These hats are worn in the Outback and the corks dangling from their brims are supposed to chase away the flies. – **47 to preclude** (v.): here: prevent s.b. from achieving s.th. – **48 to revere** (v.): feel deep respect for s.b. – **60 to contrive** (v.): plan in an elaborate way, design – **60 zeal** (n.): here: enthusiasm – **61 irreverence** (n.): feeling no respect – **64 larrikin** (n., *Australian*): here: hooligan – **74 to sack** (v.): to dismiss, fire

Explanations

Intro: Boonie: David Boon (born 29 December 1960, Launceston, Tasmania), a great Tasmanian cricketer who wants to become the first Australian president. He has got his own website (www.boonieforpresident.com) on which he proclaims: "The Queen is dead, Long Live President Boonie." – **4 Fosters**: famous Australian brand of beer – **30 Snowy Mountains**: range of mountains in NSW, near Canberra – **32 Robert Hughes**: Australian writer and art critic who lives in America, author of "The Real Australia," *Time*, Magazine Archives, 156, 12 (18 September 2000) – **36 King Zog of Albania**: originally Ahmed Bey Zogy, an Albanian chieftain. He ruled Albania for 14 years, first as president (1925-28), then as King Zog I (1928-39).

Awareness

1 When was the (British) Commonwealth of Nations founded and which nations have joined, left or rejoined since then?

Comprehension

2 Why do most people think it's ridiculous that Australians still have the Queen of England as head of state?
3 Which differences are there according to Chancellor between Australians and the US-Americans?

Analysis

4 Why are Australians afraid of having a politician as head of state?
5 What does the writer refer to when he speaks of the "jolly swagman's irreverence for symbols of authority and privilege?" (ll. 61–63)
6 Read "The Real Australia" (see explanations on p. 45) and compare the ways in which Hughes and Chancellor treat the topic of monarchy.

Opinion

7 The author writes: "Whatever happens today will not be the end of the story" (ll. 78f.). How do you think Australians will deal with the problem of who should be head of state in the future?

Project

8 Write an amendment to the Australian constitution which lays down a procedure for electing an Australian president.

Info

Australia's first female Prime Minister – a Welsh immigrant

On 24 June 2010, after only two and a half years in office, Kevin Rudd stepped down as Prime Minister of Australia. He was succeeded by Julia Gillard, the new leader of the Labor Party.

Ms Gillard was not born in Australia but in Barry, a small town in Wales. When she was five, her working class parents decided to emigrate to Australia. They were drawn by promises of employment and housing, a more relaxed lifestyle and a better climate. In those days the Australian government tried to attract more white people from Commonwealth countries by means of the so-called "Ten Pound Pom" scheme, a programme of assisted migration ("Pom" is a rather derogatory word for people from Great Britain). Adult migrants were charged £10 for their fare and children travelled for free. In 1966 the Gillards arrived in Adelaide where Julia went to high school and later studied law and arts at the local university. As a student she was politically active and became the National President of the Australian Union of Students in 1983. After her final examination she worked as an industrial lawyer but also pursued a political career which took shape in 1998 when she won a seat in Parliament. She became Deputy Prime Minister after Kevin Rudd's election victory in 2007.

The fact that at the moment the two most important political offices – Head of State and Prime Minister – are held by women who were not born in Australia shows how relaxed Australians feel about such things as nationalism, national pride or national identity.

16 Greenpeace

Faking It

The greenhouse effect, where industrial gases such as carbon dioxide trap the sun's heat in the upper atmosphere, is now seen as the principal cause of global warming. As a result weather conditions will become more extreme. Deserts will grow and there will be severe storms and disastrous floods. Global warming affects the whole world but it is mainly caused by the industrialised west including Australia, where bushfires, droughts and floods have increased over the last years. Greenpeace takes a critical look at what Australia does to tackle this problem. - Taken from the internet: Greenpeace Australia Pacific, Australian Conservation Foundation, Friends of the Earth, *Faking It* (ISBN 1 876221 11 9).

As concern grows over the environmental and economic threats posed by human-induced climate change, the Australian Government has intensified its attempts to create an image of a progressive country with a comprehensive range of climate change policies. In truth, as this report shows, Australia's greenhouse performance is shameful.

Sometimes, congested traffic pollutes the air in Sydney

Not satisfied with bullying the rest of the world into allowing Australia an 8% increase in emissions under the Kyoto Protocol, the Australian Government is failing to take serious action to tackle climate change.

According to figures submitted to the Intergovernmental Panel on Climate Change (IPCC), Australia is among the highest per capita greenhouse emitters in the world. Per capita emissions are almost twice the industrialised country average of 13.4 tonnes. In 1998 emissions excluding landclearing increased to 116.9% of 1990 levels – well beyond Australia's + 8% Kyoto target.

This contrasts sharply with countries like Germany, which has reduced emissions by 17%. In the last two years the United Kingdom, Denmark, India and China have all achieved reductions. Denmark and the United Kingdom have already achieved reductions equal to their Kyoto targets.

Despite the government trumpeting that it has spent $1 billion on greenhouse, action in Australia amounts to an elaborate smoke-and-mirrors exercise. Rather than confronting the problem head-on, the government relies on voluntary initiatives that have failed to move the nation beyond business as usual. Emissions rates from transport and electricity consumption have *accelerated* since Australia signed the Kyoto Protocol and the government has admitted, that even with measures already introduced, it expects emissions in the first commitment period to be 18–20% above 1990 levels.

Unwilling to take any serious action, the Australian Government is relying on loopholes in the Kyoto Protocol to meet its target. Risky sinks schemes, deceptive 'renewable' energy proposals and dubious technology transfers to the developing world could potentially allow Australia to meet its Kyoto commitments 'on paper' while industrial pollution continues to rise.

This report, a joint analysis by Greenpeace Australia, Friends of the Earth and the Australian Conservation Foundation, shows that, contrary to the honest broker image the government attempts to portray, when it comes to genuine action on climate change, Australia is faking it.

Conclusion

It is a short-sighted agenda. The cost to Australia of not taking serious action to tackle climate change is high. Recent modelling shows the impacts of climate change on Australia include:

- increased intensity and frequency of coral bleaching leading to annual bleaching events on the Great Barrier Reef by 2030–2070, threatening the survival of the reef itself and a tourism industry worth $2 billion a year;
- significant changes to rainfall patterns, exacerbating both floods and droughts;
- insufficient snow for viable operations at most ski resorts by 2070;
- the loss of up to 20% of all species in south-eastern Australia;
- major negative impacts on agriculture, including reduced milk yields, a 138% increase in heat stress on beef cattle and rapidly declining wheat yields resulting from temperature increases and decreased rainfall.

> "Never before in Australian history have we been confronted with such destruction at the hands of fire. [Governments should ...] follow scientific advice and keep firefighters and the community safe by halving the country's greenhouse gas emissions by 2020."
> *Peter Marshall, National Secretary of the United Firefighters, 11 February 2009, www.greenpeace.org.au.*

Vocabulary

Title: to fake (v.): to pretend to be s.th. one is not – **2 to pose** (v.): here: to create – **10 to bully** (v.): to threaten to hurt s.o.or frighten them, esp. s.o. who is weaker – **19 per capita** (n.): by heads; for each person – **24 landclearing** (n.): the destruction of native vegetation, e.g. the bulldozing of native bushlands, forests, savannah woodlands and grasslands – **35 smoke-and-mirrors exercise** (n.): s.th. intended to disguise or draw attention away from s.th. (esp. from s.th. embarrassing) – **45 loophole** (n.): possibility of avoiding s.th. because the words of a contract are not clear – **46 sinks** (n., pl.): processes which remove greenhouse gases from the atmosphere, e.g. growing forests – **57 honest broker**: a person who tries to get other people to reach an agreement – **74 to exacerbate** (v.): to make worse, aggravate – **76 viable** (adj.): possible – **81 milk yields** (n.): the amount of milk that is produced

Explanations

Title: Greenpeace: An independent organisation which intends to expose global environmental problems – **13 Kyoto Protocol**: The United Nations Framework Convention on Climate Change, or Global Warming Convention, was one of the main documents agreed upon at the Earth Summit, a conference held at Rio de Janeiro, Brazil (14 June 1992). The Kyoto Protocol is an amendment to this treaty on climate change. The countries which signed this protocol have agreed to reduce their greenhouse gas emissions. – **18 IPCC**: The Intergovernmental Panel on Climate Change was established by the United Nations Environmental Programme (UNEP) in 1988 to assess the information relevant for the understanding of human induced climate change and its potential impacts on the environment. – **42 first commitment period** (n.): time by which a number of promised goals (of reduction) must be achieved, here: 2008-2012 – **54 Friends of the Earth**: a worldwide federation of environmental organisations from 70 countries (2010) – **55 Australian Conservation Foundation (AFC)**: a democratic, membership-based organisation that works towards a society which protects, sustains and restores the environment – **69 coral bleaching** (n.): the dying of corals because of changes in the reef environment. Even slight changes in water temperature (1-2 degrees C) make certain (coloured) parts of reef-building corals vulnerable to damage by light.

Greenhouse Gas Emissions (tons per capita)

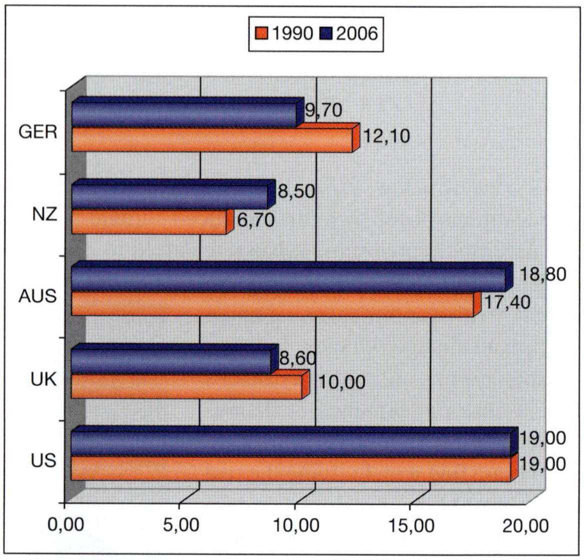

Source: US Department of Energy's Carbon Dioxide Information Analysis Center (CDIAC), based on data collected by the United Nations Statistics Division

Awareness

1 What are the most serious environmental problems Germany has to deal with at present?
2 What is the "greenhouse effect"?

Comprehension

3 According to Greenpeace the Australian Government is failing to take any serious action to tackle the problem of climate change. How do they support their contention?

Analysis

4 Explain what consequences the following problems have on the people living in the areas affected: a) coral bleaching; b) changing rainfall patterns; c) insufficient snowfall in ski resorts; d) loss of animal species.
5 Compare the greenhouse gas emissions of Australia, the United States and Germany. Calculate the percentage of change for each year. With the help of your findings prove or disprove what Greenpeace says in the text.
6 Present your figures in a graph or diagram in order to illustrate their meaning.

Opinion

7 The Australian government claims that it has implemented measures which support a sustainable development. Write a letter to the editor of a newspaper suggesting what Australians should do to achieve sustainable development.

Projects

8 Collect information on changes that might be linked to the greenhouse effect. Put them together in a reader which you may present to other groups at your school.

9 An environmentalist from Greenpeace and a politician representing people in an industrial area are invited to give their opinions on a radio programme. Write down what they say.

10 Search the internet for a class at an Australian school with which you may discuss environmental concerns. The following address may help you: http://www.edunet.ie/links/aus.html.

17 Tim Flannery

"Whoever owns the fuel"

Wildfires are common in Australia during the summer, but in 2009 they were particularly bad. More than 2000 homes were destroyed, and 210 people died in February when after years of drought the state of Victoria was struck by fierce bushfires which are considered as Australia's worst natural disaster of modern times. Later that year new fires broke out on the west coast near Perth destroying houses and consuming 33,000 acres of land. – Tim Flannery, "Whoever owns the fuel", *The Guardian*, Wednesday 11 February 2009, p. 31.

Arson is suspected, but Australians must accept pollution and unbridled growth are firebugs too.

The day after the great fire burned through central Victoria, I drove from Sydney to Melbourne. Smoke obscured the horizon, entering my air-conditioned car and carrying with it that distinctive scent so strongly signifying death, or, to Aboriginal people, cleansing.

It was as if a great cremation had taken place. I didn't know then how many people had died in their cars and homes, or while fleeing, but by the time I reached the scorched ground just north of Melbourne, the dreadful news was trickling in. Australia has suffered its worst recorded peacetime loss of life. And the trauma will be with us for ever.

I was born in Victoria, and over five decades I've watched as the state has changed. The long, wet and cold winters that seemed insufferable to me as a boy vanished decades ago, and for the last 12 years a new, drier climate has established itself. I could measure its progress whenever I flew in to Melbourne. Over the years the farm dams filled less frequently while the suburbs crept further into the countryside, their swimming pools oblivious to the great drying.

Climate modelling suggests the decline of southern Australia's winter rainfall is caused by a build-up of greenhouse gas, much of it from coal burning. Victoria has the most polluting coal power plant on earth, and another plant was threatened by the fire. There's evidence that global pollution caused a significant change in climate after the huge El Niño event of 1998. Along with the dwindling rainfall has come a desiccation of the soil, and more extreme summer temperatures.

This February, at the zenith of a record-breaking heatwave, Melbourne recorded its hottest day ever – a suffocating 46.1 °C, with even higher temperatures in rural Victoria. This extreme coincided with exceptionally strong northerly winds, followed by an abrupt change to southerly. This brought a cooling, but it was the shift in wind direction that caught so many in a deadly trap. Such conditions have occurred before. In 1939 and 1983 they led to dangerous fires. But this time the conditions were more extreme than they had ever been, and the 12-year "drought" meant plant tissues were bone dry.

Despite narrowly missing the 1983 Victorian fires and then losing a house to the 1994 Sydney bushfires, I had not previously appreciated the difference a degree or two of additional heat and a dry soil can make to the ferocity of a fire. This fire was quantitatively different from anything seen before.

My country is still in shock at the loss of so many lives. But inevitably we will look for lessons from this natural tragedy. The first, I fear, is that we must anticipate more such terrible blazes, for the world's addiction to burning fossil fuels goes on unabated. And there is now no doubt that emissions pollution is laying the preconditions necessary for more such blazes.

When he ratified the Kyoto protocol, Australia's prime minister, Kevin Rudd, described climate change as the greatest threat facing humanity. Shaken, and clearly having seen things none of us should see, he has now had the eyewitness proof of his words. We can only hope Australia's climate policy, which is weak, is now significantly strengthened.

Rudd has said the arsonists suspected of lighting some fires are guilty of mass murder, and the police are pursuing the malefactors. But there's an old saying among Australian firefighters: "Whoever owns the fuel owns the fire." Let's hope Australians ponder the deeper causes of this horrible event, and change their polluting ways before it's too late.

A bushfire – what are the causes?

Vocabulary

1 arson (n.): the crime of deliberately making something burn - **2 unbridled** (adj.): not controlled and too extreme or violent - **2 firebugs** (n., infml.) persons who deliberately set fire to a property - **7 cleansing** (v.): removing everything that is bad or immoral, making s.th. completely clean - **31 dwindling** (v.): gradually becoming less or smaller - **31 desiccation** (n.): the process of becoming completely dry - **48 ferocity** (n.): the state of being extremely violent - **54 unabated** (adj.): continuing without becoming any weaker or less violent - **66 malefactor** (n.): someone who does bad or illegal things - **68 ponder** (v.): spend time thinking carefully and seriously about a problem

Explanations

Intro: Tim Flannery: a scientist at the University of Macquarie, Sydney. He was honoured in 2005 as "Australian Humanist of the Year" and he was named "Australian of the Year" in 2007. - **30 El Niño**: name of an abnormal warming of surface ocean waters in the South Pacific. It has an impact on weather conditions throughout the world and also affects marine life (cf. text 16, ll. 69 ff.: coral bleaching). - **44 1983 Victorian fires**: On February 16, 1983 over 100 fires swept across Victoria and South Australia, killing 75 people and causing widespread damage. - **45 1994 Sydney bushfires**: In 1994 the Eastern Seaboard fires surrounded Sydney. Highways out of the city were cut off and trains were unable to run because of the fires. - **57 Kyoto Protocol**: cf. text 16, explanations - **58 Kevin Rudd:** cf. text 3

Awareness

1 Collect important facts about the great wildfires of 2009 in Melbourne, Athens and Los Angeles. You will find help on the website of *World Disaster Wildfire Timeline*.

Comprehension

2 Which changes did the writer notice over the last five decades in the state of Victoria?
3 In which way was the fire of 2009 different from the ones before?

Analysis

4 Describe the conditions which, according to the text, may lead to an outbreak of bushfires.
5 Flannery contends that the first lesson to be learned from this great fire is that Australians must "anticipate more such blazes" (ll. 52f.). Explain why this is of so great importance.
6 The headline quotes an old saying. What does the writer emphasise by means of this quotation?

Opinion

7 How do you think can pollution and unbridled growth be responsible for bushfires?
8 Some of the fires are suspected to have been lit deliberately, others were caused by gross negligence. How should the state react to such crimes?

Project

9 Develop a statistical survey of the development of bushfires in Australia. The statistics should at least include casualties, injured persons, damaged property and burnt area.

18 Australian cuisine

Martin Arndt

Australian cuisine has been shaped by the people who settled in Australia. The waves of immigration to Australia from various nations across the world have historically played an important role in shaping the direction of modern Australian cuisine. Among the English immigrants were sheep graziers providing prime lamb, others farmed beef cattle and still others became the butchers, bakers and candlestick makers of newly established towns. Many of their recipes still hold their place in home cooking of today including lamb roast, Lamingtons or steak and kidney pies.

Damper: a traditional Australian (bush) bread going back to both Aboriginal and White Australian cooking. It was originally developed by stockmen who travelled in remote areas for weeks or months at a time, with only basic rations of flour, sugar and tea, supplemented by whatever meat was available. The damper was normally cooked in the ashes of the camp fire. The ashes were flattened and the damper was placed in there for ten minutes to cook. Following this, the damper was covered with ashes and cooked for another 20 to 30 minutes until the damper sounded hollow when tapped. Alternatively, the damper was cooked in a greased camp oven.

Kangaroo meat: Kangaroo is part of the food choices, but is not popular with all Australians (see Info below).

Fish and seafood: Australia's favourable climate has also made barbecues a commonplace event at gatherings of friends and families. Barbecues are also common in fund raising for schools and local communities, where sausages and cooked onion are served on white bread with tomato sauce or Barbecue sauce (for recipes see http://www.recipesource.com/ethnic/asia/australian).

Recent developments: Recently Australians have thrown off the British yoke of pub grub and have embraced the great bounty from their own seas along with home-grown fruit and vegetables and the spices of Asia, like e.g. in the high quality *Boilerhouse Harbourside Restaurant – Quarantine Station*, situated on the edge of Sydney's amazing harbourside (http://www.qstation.com.au/). For 140 years the *Quarantine Station* was used to house newly arrived immigrants and for this reason it is an important part of the history of Australia. Gradually buildings were added to the complex and these buildings reflect the beliefs and practices of the times in which they were built. In 1984 the Quarantine Station became part of the Sydney Harbour National Park under the management of the National Parks and Wildlife Service who set up a guided tour and interpretation service for visitors.

Info

Australian cuisine vocabulary

- Bangers: sausages
- bangers and mash – sausages and mashed potato
- billy tea – bush tea boiled in a tin container
- booze – alcohol
- bundy – Bundaberg rum, e.g. 'bundy and coke'
- bushfood (also called bush tucker) – any food native to Australia and used as sustenance by the original inhabitants, the Australian Aborigines. Examples of Australian native animal food (meat) include kangaroo, emu and crocodile. In particular, kangaroo is quite common and can be found in many normal supermarkets at prices comparable to beef. Other animals, for example goanna and witchetty grubs, were eaten by Aboriginal Australians and thus qualify as bushfood in every sense of the word. Fish and shellfish are culinary features of the Australian coastal communities.
- champers – champagne
- chook – chicken
- grog – alcohol
- Lamingtons – a traditional sponge cake
- lollies – candy
- middy – medium sized glass of beer
- sanga – sandwich
- schooner – large glass of beer
- snag – sausage
- stubby – small bottle of beer
- tinny – can of beer
- tomato sauce – ketchup
- tucker – food

NEW ZEALAND

Ninety Mile Beach
Bay of Islands
Paihia
Auckland
Bay of Plenty
North Island
Rotorua
Lake Taupo
Taupo
Napier
Tasman Sea
Cook Strait
Picton
Nelson
Wellington
Pacific Ocean
Greymouth
Harihari
Christchurch
Lake Wanaka
Timaru
Lake Hawea
South Island
Queenstown
Lake Te Anau
Dunedin
Otago
Stewart Island

"Aotearoa – Land of the Long White Cloud"

New Zealand is an end-of-the-earth sort of place, a pair of islands and associated islets lifted to their present heights, after an adventuresome geological career, as recently as five million years ago. With Patagonia and southern Chile, it is the southernmost land area in the world, quite appropriately the base for the (...) U.S. Navy's explorations of Antarctica, whose shores lie fifteen hundred miles to the south. New Zealanders say that London is halfway between New Zealand and New Zealand – in other words it is about twelve thousand miles away no matter whether you go northeast or northwest.

New Zealand's land area is 103,736 square miles: it compares in size with Italy. Of the two main islands, the South Island is the bigger by about fourteen thousand square miles. But whereas the South Island is roughly a long rectangle, the North Island is looped and pronged with bays and peninsulas. The combined lengths of the two islands are about a thousand miles, and (...) the shoreline, indentations and all, measures just short of ten thousand miles. The dividing water is Cook Strait – once again a name drawn from the stalwart British captain who first closely explored these waters. It is narrow, less than twenty miles, yet with tumultuous seas. Auckland lies in the north of that island, and Wellington, the capital, is on the southern tip of it. The North Island has more than two-thirds of New Zealand's population, which is pushing three million. It also has more than half of the nation's sixty million sheep. Incidentally, domestic animals, including cattle, outnumber human beings in New Zealand by twenty-five to one, a ratio probably not exceeded by any other country in the world.

Quoted from: John Gunther, *Inside Australia and New Zealand*, ed. William N. Forbis (London: Hamilton, 1972), pp. 286 ff.

Vocabulary

islet (n.): small island – **looped** (adj.): curved – **pronged** (adj.): having pointed parts at the end like e.g. a fork – **indentation** (n.): zigzag – **stalwart** (adj.): robust, resolute – **to push** (v.): to reach, to come close to – **ratio** (n.): relation between two amounts

Explanations

Aotearoa (n.): in the language of the native New Zealanders: land of the long white cloud – **Patagonia**: a region of South America, belonging to southern Argentina and Chile, consisting largely of a dry barren plateau, extending from the Colorado river in central Argentina to the Strait of Magellan and from the Andes to the Atlantic coast – **Cook Strait**: the passage of water that separates the North and South islands of New Zealand – **Auckland**: originally the trading post in a populous Maori district (Maori: member of the Aboriginal race of New Zealand), it became the site of the first Parliament and remained the capital of New Zealand until 1865. It expanded into an industrial and commercial centre, thus becoming the largest city and chief seaport of New Zealand. – **Wellington**: planned in 1840 by the New Zealand Company and founded by Edward Gibbon Wakefield (1796–1862) with the aim of colonising the country, it became the capital in 1865. It was named after the Duke of Wellington (1769–1852) who defeated Napoleon at the Battle of Waterloo in 1815.

19

John Gunther

"Early History and Discovery" *

The early (Polynesian) period of New Zealand's history can be divided into an early "archaic" (AD 800 or even earlier) and a later "classic" (AD 1100 or later) phase. The first Polynesians lived mainly on the South Island where they found moas (flightless birds), which became their major food supply. The "classic" Maori encountered later by Cook were agriculturalists most of whom lived in the warmer northern parts of the country. It is these people whom John Gunther describes. - John Gunther, *Inside Australia and New Zealand*, ed. William N. Forbis (London: Hamilton, 1972), pp. 129 ff.

Early History

New Zealand's prehistory is a maddening mixture of firm facts, probabilities, and contradictory mysteries. A probability is that the Polynesians were originally Asian Caucasoid, modified by Mongoloid and Negroid blood as they moved eastward through Indonesia and Melanesia to the Pacific islands of Hawaii, Tahiti, and Easter Island. Certain it is that they became good canoemen, capable of sailing at least a few hundred miles, well out of sight of land, in canoes that could carry 250 people. Certain it is, too, that their canoes began to take them to New Zealand more than a thousand years ago.

The pre-Pakeha civilization of the Maoris, a handsome people of light brown skin, was the highest in Polynesia.

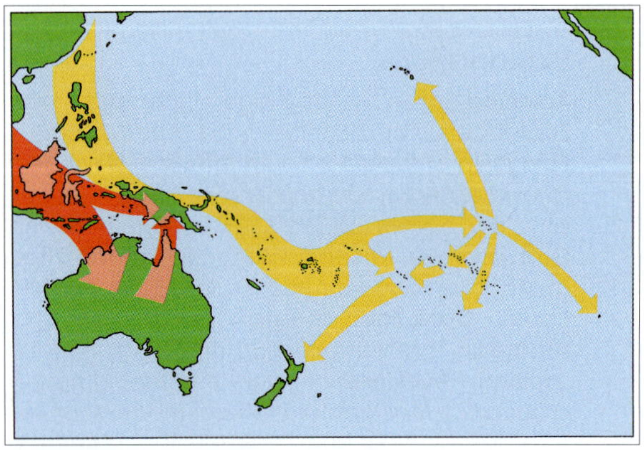

Polynesian migration

They were an agricultural people, artistic, religious, and warlike. For adzes and clubs, they crossed the Southern Alps to the West Coast for a kind of translucent jade known in New Zealand as greenstone. They built, on numerous hilltops, a kind of conical fortress called a pa. They found flax growing in New Zealand, and learned to make it into baskets and clothing. For meeting houses and the prows of canoes, they practiced wood carving that ranks high in primitive art.

Day-to-day life revolved around the cultivation of the sweet potato, the taro root, and the yam. For other food they ate fern roots, birds, fish, and one another. The Maoris were notorious cannibals, keeping people in pens to fatten them up, and eating all shipwrecked sailors. Tribal organization was based on the family, then the subtribe, with a common ancestor, and finally the tribe, with a set of distant common ancestors who, according to legend, would have all arrived in the same canoe. The canoes, incidentally, all have names, and to this day it is common for a Maori to speak of descent from the Tainui canoe, or the Te Arawa canoe, or the Tokomaru canoe. The characteristics of the religion were, first, many gods but no supreme god, and secondly, a powerful sense of tapu (the origin of the English word "taboo"), which served to enforce customs and the law.

Discovery

James Cook, with Sir Joseph Banks and his party, sailed around both islands of New Zealand in 1769 and 1770, and mapped them. Cook landed in two places, taking possession of the islands in the name of King George III, but he found the native Maoris fierce, warlike and unfriendly, and did not stay. Between 1770 and 1779, Cook made four other visits. The French also sent expeditions to New Zealand in 1769 and 1772. During the second expedition their leader Du Fresne and many of his men were killed by the Maoris.

Ships from Sydney made visits to New Zealand soon after the foundation of New South Wales. The first settlers were escaped convicts and bushrangers who had made the dangerous journey from New South Wales at about the turn of the century, often in small boats which they had stolen. Some were carried in ships by sympathetic sailors. These men were sometimes disreputable characters and they taught the Maoris to use rum and firearms. Some intermarried with the Maoris and tried to build up small private kingdoms. One French adventurer actually called himself King of New Zealand in 1822. By 1839 there were some 2,000 white men of mixed race in New Zealand.

The first British missionaries arrived in 1814 under Samuel Marsden and many others followed. They had a tremendous influence on the Maoris who were a very intelligent race, many becoming Christian. Later, from 1842 to 1869, Bishop Selwyn did a great deal to civilise the natives. [...]

The settlement began at the spot which is now Wellington. The British Government was forced to act, and Captain William Hobson, a naval officer, was sent from Sydney to act as lieutenant governor under the Governor of New South Wales. In November of 1840 New Zealand became a separate colony and Hobson became governor. Auckland was the first capital although it was replaced by Wellington in 1865. Once again, as in New South Wales, a naval officer quite arbitrarily selected proved an outstanding governor.

The feared French expedition arrived off Akaroa in 1840, but Captain Hobson sent Captain Stanley to forestall them. The French expedition sailed away but a few French remained as colonists under British rule.

At Waitangi the same year, Hobson called a great gathering of Maori chiefs. In the Treaty of Waitangi which followed the chiefs recognised the Great White Queen across the seas; Hobson guaranteed them British protection; the Maori land rights were recognised; it was agreed that they should sell land only to the Government and not to individual settlers or to the New Zealand Company; all land was to be paid for and to be sold only by the tribe as a whole. Hobson had a great understanding of the Maori and certainly won their confidence. The Treaty was very much in their favour and was resented by the New Zealand Company who wished to purchase land cheaply and were guilty of violation of the Treaty in the years which followed. The Maoris, who were of high intelligence, fully understood the Treaty and its failure to work entirely as intended was because of a misunderstanding of the Maori system of holding land. Their land did not belong to the chiefs but to the whole tribe and this made for great difficulty. With both the Company and individual settlers buying land from the Maoris in defiance of the Treaty and some land being sold several times by the same tribe, chaos ensued. In spite of a special Commissioner being sent from Britain to settle the land question, disputes went on for some years. This made the Wakefield system more difficult to put into operation because of the difficulty of fixing a price for land and the fact that no emigration fund could be set up. Nevertheless, it was a successful colony in spite of the early troubles.

Vocabulary

16 adze (n.): a tool for cutting away the surface of wood, like an axe - **17 translucent** (adj.): allowing light to pass through - **19 conical** (adj.): shaped like a cone: with a circular plane base and the thickness gradually diminishing to its tip - **20 flax** (n.): a blue-flowered plant, cultivated for its textile fibre and its seed - **22 prow** (n.): the fore-part of a boat or ship - **25 taro** (n.): tropical plant, used as food in many countries - **25 yam** (n.): a tropical plant - **26 fern** (n.): a type of plant with green leaves shaped like large feathers, but no flowers - **27 pen** (n.): a small prison-like building, normally used for cows, sheep and poultry - **30 subtribe**: smaller unit of a tribe - **57 sympathetic** (adj.): showing sympathy and understanding - **58 disreputable** (adj.): having a bad reputation - **59 to intermarry** (v.): to become connected by marriage - **79 outstanding** (adj.): extremely good - **82 to forestall** (v.): to act in advance of in order to prevent or stop s.th.

Explanations

Intro: Polynesian: a native or inhabitant of Polynesia, the region of the central Pacific - **Intro: Maori**: member of the Polynesian aboriginal people of New Zealand - **5 Caucasoid**: relating to the Caucasian division of humankind and referring to the light-skinned branch that was believed to have been originated in the Caucasus region of southeast Europe - **5 Mongoloid**: relating to the division of humankind including the indigenous peoples of eastern Asia, southeast Asia and the arctic region of North America - **5 Negroid**: characterising a member of the black group of human populations - **6 Melanesia**: region of the western Pacific, lying south of the equator - **7 Easter Island**: an island in the southeast Pacific west of Chile - **13 Pakeha**: Maori name for the white person as opposed to Maori - **16 Southern Alps**: mountain range in South Island, extending for almost the entire length of the island - **35 Tainui/Te Arawa/Tokomaru**: names of traditional Maori canoe - **38 tapu**: Maori word for s.th. set apart as sacred or prohibited - **41 Sir Joseph Banks**: British explorer and naturalist (1743–1820) who accompanied James Cook - **49 Marc-Joseph Marion du Fresne**: French explorer of the 18th century - **65 Samuel Marsden**: Marsden (1765–1838), originally a priest of the Church of England, was the founder of missions in New Zealand, although he never settled there. - **68 Bishop Selwyn**: George Augustus Selwyn (1809–1878) was the first bishop of New Zealand in 1841, saying prayers and preaching in Maori. - **72 William Hobson**: born in Ireland (1793), he joined the royal navy and later became the first governor of New Zealand and the founder of Auckland. He died at an early age (1842). He is especially known for signing the treaty of Waitangi. - **80 Akaroa**: harbour on the east coast of South Island south of Christchurch

Awareness

1 Look at the photos in your book that show parts of New Zealand. What information on her can you conclude from them?

Comprehension

2 List what information on the history of the Maoris the article provides the reader with.

Analysis

3 Do the stylistic devices used in the text prove the author's assertion that "New Zealand's prehistory is a maddening mixture of firm facts, probabilities, and contradictory mysteries" (ll. 2f.)? If so, give examples.
4 Find out the differences between the Australian Aboriginals' and the Maoris' attempts to find a new country where to settle.

Opinion

5 Imagine you were a Maori – how would you present the history of the Maoris in order to cast a favourable light on your kinsmen?

Projects

6 Design a chart that illustrates the ethnic composition of New Zealand.
7 Create an attractive front page for a tourist catalogue on New Zealand.

20 Jim Bolger

"Waitangi Day Commemorations, 1995"

The Rt Hon Jim Bolger was Prime Minister of New Zealand from October 1990 to December 1997. He led the National Party for almost 12 years and had three consecutive terms as the country's head of government. The following text is an extract of his speech on Waitangi Day Commemorations, celebrated annually on February 6 and recognised as New Zealand's national day. He considers the treaty as fundamental to the relationship between the Crown and the Maori people. – Jim Bolger, "Waitangi Day Commemorations, 1995", speech given on 5 February, 1995, New Zealand Executive Government Speech Archive.

E nga mana, a n a reo, e nga hau e wha, tena koutou.
To the many holders of mana, the many voices, to the four winds, greetings.

E n a tini aitua, tini mate, haere, haere, haere, haere, atu ra.
To those who have passed before us, farewell.

1 [...] The treaty was a pragmatic solution to the dramatic changes that had occurred in New Zealand with the arrival of the Europeans. Both parties acknowledged that they needed to work together. It was not a time to bemoan the past but rather to prepare for a future both sides knew was going to be very different from what had gone before.

During our time of stewardship, my Government has committed considerable time and energy to building on the legacy our ancestors left us. In the year just passed, we put together a settlement package to settle honourably and honestly the land grievances our nation has lived for so long. Some of you have acknowledged our approach and said, let's sit down and talk about the details. Others didn't like it at all and said rather than talking with us they would march in Wellington, no doubt shouting slogans. In my view the time for shouting is past. It is time for serious talk. [...]

1995 is Maori Language Year. New Zealand has two official languages, Maori and English. The English language was one of the great gifts that the early settlers brought to New Zealand. It is a language that is taught and used around the world – it is the main language of international commerce and the main language of the computer.

Tonight however I want to speak of the Maori language. Of why it is important that all New Zealanders make an effort to appreciate its beauty and its importance to New Zealand. It is important because it is unique, it is part of New Zealand, not only yesterday, but today and tomorrow. Meet a group of New Zealanders anywhere around the world and ask them to sing a song of home and most will sing *Po kare kare ana*.

Singing one song in Maori is not enough. I want to see the time when all primary schools in New Zealand teach sufficient Maori to children so they all feel comfortable with their second official language. I want to see a New Zealand in which we all love the two languages of our nation – Maori and English. I know that won't happen tomorrow. But the 21st century is almost upon us. Let's make progress towards that goal. Pakeha children will find in Maori a language that speaks of the very dearest things of our nation. They will also find a language that is no mere museum piece, but continually growing, adapting to new realities. For Maori, proper recognition of their language will be an acknowledgement that we respect their contribution to what makes New Zealand unique.

Language of course is about dialogue. About understanding each other.

The Maori at Waitangi made high efforts to speak the language of the Pakeha who arrived on their shores. And many of the newcomers strove to speak the language they encountered. Both peoples sought to communicate, not just in words, but in concepts. Together, they agreed to try to make a nation based on common laws and common institutions. Some who call themselves activists, I venture to say, have forgotten that. We should not be diverted by them. We should not allow them to drive a wedge between the people of our nation.

1994 was a good year for all New Zealanders. The economy grew and there were many more jobs. A very serious commitment was made to resolve past land issues. The Government's offer is on the table and we are willing to talk. 155 years ago two peoples came to Waitangi to map out a new way of living together. We are still doing our best. With a little understanding, a little aroha, we can make it.

Maori life in the 21st century

Today is again a tune for us to readdress what it is to be a New Zealander. It is not a time for guilt not anger, it is not a time for recrimination and frustration. For many New Zealanders today is just another holiday, a time for sport, family and relaxation. Here, today, though it is important that we rededicate ourselves to persuade all our people, Maori and non-Maori, to focus on a future where we share common goals, a real sense of ourselves and unique heritage.

Ma te Atua tatou katos, hei manaaka, hei tiaki.

May the Lord care for and guide us all.

Tena koutou, tena koutou, tena koutou katoa.

Greetings, greetings, thrice greetings.

Vocabulary

Intro: Rt Hon (abbr.): Right Honourable (used when formally announcing or talking about a British member of Parliament) - **Intro: to pass** (v.): to die - **5 to bemoan** (v.): to complain about - **8 stewardship** (n.): administrative responsibility - **12 grievance** (n.): complaint - **53 to strive** (v.): strove/striven: to try hard - **58 to venture** (v.): to take risks, to do s.th. that requires courage - **59 to divert** (v.): to draw the attention of - **60 to drive a wedge between people**: to make people become enemies - **71 recrimination** (n.): second accusation made after s.o. made the first one

Explanations

Intro: Jim Bolger: James Brendan Bolger (born in 1935) became Prime Minister of New Zealand in 1990. - **Intro: mana**: Maori word for power and prestige - **1 treaty**: referring to the treaty of Waitangi signed in 1840 by which most northern Maori chiefs agreed to accept British rule and the British Government guaranteed to protect the Maoris, especially in the possession of their lands, against colonists. The land was recognised as Maori property which could only be transferred through the British Crown. The treaty is still of central importance when the relations between the Maoris and the Pakehas (Whites) are discussed. - **33 Po kare kare ana**: famous Maori song

Awareness

1 What special days are commemorated in your country?

Comprehension

2 Why does Bolger call the treaty of Waitangi a "pragmatic solution" (l. 1)?
3 What is meant by Bolger's statement that "both peoples sought to communicate, not just in words, but in concepts" (ll. 54f.)?

Analysis

4 Determine the effect of the stylistic devices Bolger uses in order to convey his message.
5 Why does Bolger distance himself from some groups?
6 Find out which elements Bolger considers to be vital parts of a New Zealander identity.

Opinion

7 Do you think that governments should still spend taxes on preserving languages of minorities in a globalising world of "international commerce and [...] computer" (ll. 24f.)?
8 If you were living abroad, would you stand up for the right to speak your native language?
9 Bolger admires pragmatism and quotes from religious Maori songs. Do you think that a pragmatist can simultaneously be devout?

Project

10 Find out if Bolger's goal of increasing the number of primary schools teaching "sufficient Maori to children" has, at least partially, been implemented in practice.

21

Craig Harrison

Tomorrow Will Be a Lovely Day

Craig Harrison (*1942 in Leeds, Yorkshire) is a dramatist whose plays are often set in New Zealand and focus on Maori issues, e.g. in his drama *The Quiet Earth* (1981). *Tomorrow Will Be a Lovely Day* (1974) is considered Harrison's main achievement. Conjecturing a situation in which two Maori extremists (the brothers Matenga and Tahu) precipitate civil war by stealing the Treaty of Waitangi and claiming their people's entrenched rights, set fire to the Maori Affairs building and take over the radio station, the drama sketches their backgrounds in terms of Vietnam, penitentiaries, and racism. In the following extract of the drama the Maori Matenga visits the Morleys whose daughter Sharon he has fallen in love with. – Craig Harrison, *Tomorrow will be a Lovely Day* (Auckland: Longman, 1975), pp. 13 ff.

SCENE 4

Lights have faded; stage has been changed to a New Zealand living room. Black modern paintings on walls; white rugs; cane chairs; a lamp, a spinning wheel in the corner, a record player, some earthenware pots and ashtrays.

Enter Bob and Joyce Morley.

JOYCE: Well I have no objections to Sharon going out with this Maori boy. Did you expect me to object?

BOB: No, of course not. I have nothing against Maoris. I'm not prejudiced in any way. If they wanted to get married, I'd say, fine, go ahead.

JOYCE: Marriage isn't very fashionable these days.

BOB: It seems to have a reasonable survival rate here in bourgeois Dunedin.

JOYCE: Yes, people can get tax rebates if they make their relationship legal.

Doorbell rings.

That'll be Matenga. I'll see if Sharon's ready.

Exits.

Bob lets Matenga in.

BOB: Come in, er, Matenga ...

MATENGA: Mat.

BOB: Mat. I'm Bob.

They shake hands. Matenga is dressed in a suit and white shirt and dark tie.

BOB: Sharon's not ready yet. Come and sit down.

They sit down.

BOB: Feel like a beer?

MATENGA: Er, no thanks, Mr er ...

BOB: Bob.

MATENGA: No thanks, Bob, I don't drink.

BOB: Really! *(Pause)* I mean ... very wise.

MATENGA: I once had some beer but I never really liked the taste of it.

Bob stands up, goes to the record player.

BOB: Put on a bit of music, eh. What do you like, Mat? Jimi Hendrix ... Nina Simone ... the Supremes?

MATENGA: You don't have any Martinu?

BOB: Er ...?

MATENGA: Bohuslav Martinu. The Czech bloke, Concerto for Two String Orchestras with ...

BOB: No. I'm sorry.

MATENGA: Shostakovich?

BOB: Could I get you a glass of lemonade or orange juice or something?

MATENGA: A glass of milk would be fine, Mr ... er ... Bob.

Exit Bob.

Matenga hums some opening bars of Shostakovich.

Enter Joyce, Matenga stands up.

JOYCE: Hello Matenga. Or is it *tena koe*?

MATENGA: Er, hello would do, I think.

JOYCE: I'm Joyce. Sharon will be ready in two minutes.

Awkward pause.

I, er, I learnt Maori at evening classes last year.

MATENGA: It must be very, er, very interesting. Have you had much chance to speak it yet?

JOYCE: No. But we hope to be going to the North Island, East Coast, next summer. I thought I might try a bit out on you.

MATENGA: There's not much call for it in Dunedin. I reckon you know more than I do. To be honest I don't speak it myself.

JOYCE: Perhaps we all ought to learn Gaelic. *(Laughs.)* Then the Scots down here would understand us.

MATENGA: I know of a bloke who is studying Gaelic, as it happens. It's very difficult.

JOYCE: Good heavens. Really! Gaelic? Not a Maori, surely?

MATENGA: Oh, no. *(Pause)* He's a Samoan. At the University.

Enter Bob with a mug of milk and a brandy.

BOB: Mat drinks milk. *(Hands him it.)*

MATENGA: Thanks. *(Pause.)* Cheers. *(They sit down.)*

JOYCE: I'm a potter in my spare time. And I do a bit of weaving. We don't go for all these industrial manufactured things. As Bob says, we need to get back to more natural things.

Pause.

MATENGA *(looking at lamp)*: Still got the electric, eh?

JOYCE: Bob made the lamp. Out of *driftwood*. We found it on the beach.

MATENGA: Great. I used to have a spare-time job at Stimson's, the lamp shop. But they went bust last year. Must have been a good year for driftwood, eh?

BOB: The thing I admire most about the Maori way of life is the way everyone comes together at times of stress and difficulty.

MATENGA: They certainly come to my old man. He was a bit of a miser and he finished up quite well off. Got thousands in the BNZ. Our problem is keeping people away.

BOB: Ah. Money isn't everything.

MATENGA: No, but as Dad used to say, it's better than nothing.

Pause. Bob drinks brandy.

BOB: There's quite a bit of unemployment here. The trouble is, society being so unjust, those who can least afford to be out of work are hit hard.

MATENGA: Too right. Both my brothers are out of work right now.

JOYCE: Are they manual workers?

MATENGA: Yes. Rangi's a concert pianist and TaJiu's a brain surgeon.

Enter Sharon. They all stand.

BOB: I'm not sure about letting you take Sharon out. You're not like any Maori I ever read about.

MATENGA: Sorry I don't fit the anthropological image. But what about our sense of humour? Aren't Maoris supposed to have a great sense of humour?

BOB: You mean ... you were joking all the time?

MATENGA: Would it be funny if I was?

BOB *(fiercely)*: *No!*

MATENGA: Then I wasn't. Sorry, I still don't fit the Maori image.

BOB: No, you're too clever by half.

MATENGA: *Racist!*

Pause. Sharon flounces forward, takes Matenga by the hand. They leave.

Vocabulary

3 rug (n.): floor-mat - **3 cane** (n.): stem of slender palms - **15 rebate** (n.): reduction - **73 mug** (n.): a drinking-vessel, usually with a handle - **82 driftwood** (n.): wood left behind by water or wind - **85 to go bust** (v.): to become bankrupt - **119 to flounce** (v.): to move with an impatient motion

Explanations

14 Dunedin: situated in South Island, it was founded in 1848 by Scottish settlers, its name being based on the Gaelic word for Edinburgh - **37 Jimi Hendrix**: American rock guitarist and singer (1942–1970), remembered for the originality of his improvisations and for performances at the Woodstock festival in 1969 - **37 Nina Simone**: Afro-American female pop star, especially famous in the 70s and 80s - **37 The Supremes**: very successful pop-trio of the 60s and 70s, consisting of only black female singers - **43 Shostakovich**: Dmitrij Shostakovich (1906–1975), a Russian composer whose works include symphonies, operas and many chamber works - **65 Gaelic**: Celtic language spoken in Ireland and Scotland - **92 BNZ**: Board of New Zealand

Awareness

1 What could be meant by the title of Harrison's play "Tomorrow Will Be a Lovely Day"?

Comprehension

2 How do the Morleys spend their spare time?
3 List those elements that could enable the spectator (reader) to identify the Morleys' social status.

Analysis

4 Describe how the Morleys would like to be seen.
5 What is the Morleys' image of the Maoris?
6 Why is the encounter interrupted by, as the stage-direction says, an "awkward pause"?
7 Can Bob's assertion that he is not prejudiced against Maoris be trusted or is Matenga's view that he is a "racist" right?

Opinion

8 Do you think that the Morleys may be held morally responsible for the final confrontation?
9 Discuss if the dramatist Harrison is not as prejudiced as Bob Morley when creating certain images of White New Zealanders.

Projects

8 Gather information on the lifestyle of expatriates who work as e.g. aid-workers, lawyers and doctors in less developed countries.
9 Will a cross-cultural cooperation of civilisations succeed? Work on this problem by consulting Samuel Huntington's controversial book *The Clash of Civilisations*.

22

Don McKinnon

"The EU and New Zealand Partnership" *

When the United Kingdom joined the European Union in 1973, New Zealand no longer remained its main supplier of agrarian products. Since then the government has accomplished major economic restructuring, moving an agrarian economy dependent on the British market toward a more industrialized, free market economy that can compete globally and whose economic performance can be compared to that of big West European countries. Nowadays New Zealand has come to treat the European Union as one single market. In his speech on the partnership between Europe and New Zealand Don McKinnon, Minister of Foreign Affairs and Trade and Deputy Prime Minister in 1996, outlines the development of this partnership from the early seventies to the present day. - Don McKinnon (former Minister of Foreign Affairs and Trade): "European Union - New Zealand: Partnership Briefings". Speech given on 3 October 1996. Quoted from: http://www.executive.govt.nz/93-96/minister/dpm/dps0310.htm.

A partnership with Europe is exactly what we're on about. The economic picture certainly reveals just that. Our relationship with the European Union is developing in a way which allows benefits to be gained by both sides, not just New Zealand. ...

For our part, European investment in New Zealand has had very tangible benefits. Job creation has been one of them. As an example, over 3500 New Zealanders owe their employment to direct investment from France alone.

Partnership, too, is a word which conveys the way our historical relationship with Europe has developed. Our identity as a distant colony of Britain changed dramatically when following the First World War we realised we had assumed a separate identity as New Zealanders.

New Zealand's agricultural economy also includes red deer farms

That process was given a further shot in the arm during the Second World War. We didn't hesitate to participate in the defence of democracy in Europe. But threats closer to our own shores began to colour the way we viewed the world.

When Britain joined the European Community in 1973 we realised our partnership with that country, strong and vital as it was, needed to be much more diversified. The days of New Zealand as Britain's farm were gone forever.

New Zealanders looked for a new answer to the questions: Who are we? Where do we belong? I'm not sure we have a complete answer yet. But we are well on the way.

We went through a period of introspection in the 1980s, and a fair amount of South Pacific naval gazing went on. Our non-nuclear policy didn't make us an international pariah. But it didn't exactly endear us to some. Yet we stuck to our guns, and rode out the storm.

In more recent times we have focused on the Asia-Pacific region. The result has been a dramatic upsurge in trade with the economic tigers of Asia. This new trade picture led many to question whether our links with Europe are still as important as they once were.

Let me state here quite categorically Europe remains very important to us. We have been able to benefit from the spectacular growth of the Asian markets over the last twenty years or so. Our relative proximity has been a bonus in that respect. But the European market, wealthy and discriminating as it is, has remained one where our cultural affinity has stood us in good stead. In actual fact we see the two markets as complementing each other.

The lesson we have drawn is that New Zealand should never again place all its eggs in one economic basket. As any good stock broker would counsel – we're spreading the risk.

So what does Europe get out of this? Well, the first thing is that the European Union's merchandise trade alone reaps it over $4 billion a year. But significantly, Europe is finding in New Zealand a partner economy characterised by an openness unmatched virtually anywhere else in the world, and, as I've said, scope for foreign direct investment which some European companies have been quick to seize.

Recently we have been at loggerheads with France over nuclear testing. However, France was, and remains, a significant investor in New Zealand, along with the more traditional British investment. France will always play a role in the Pacific. Investment from the European Union as a whole made up nearly a fifth of total foreign direct investment in 1995.

This was less than investment from Australia, but more than from Asia. The growth in European investment clearly reflects increased confidence in the New Zealand economy. The five-year period to 1993, for example, saw spectacular growth in foreign direct investment – from $148 million to $2.3 billion.

But there are two sides to the investment picture. New Zealanders are investing in Europe too – to the tune of $640 million in 1995. This suggests Europeans are coming to view New Zealand's natural advantages for what they are – a country with a geographical location conveniently close to and linked with the Asian market.

Vocabulary

17 was given a further shot in the arm: was further encouraged - **31 introspection** (n.): the examination of one's own motives - **32 navel gazing**: being only interested in or concerned with one's own problems - **34 pariah** (n.): an outcast, not acceptable to society - **34 to endear** (v.): make s.b. loved or liked - **34f. we stuck to our guns and rode out the storm**: we survived this difficult time without changing our opinion - **37 upsurge** (n.): sudden great increase - **44 proximity** (n.): being near - **46 discriminating** (adj.): favouring or discouraging imports and exports (by means of tariffs, import duties etc.) - **47 has stood us in good stead**: was helpful to us - **48 to complement** (v.): to make complete - **52 stock broker** (n.): a person that buys and sells stocks and shares for others - **57 reaps it**: makes it gain/earn - **62 scope** (n.): here: opportunity - **66 at loggerheads**: disagreeing or quarelling - **81f. to the tune of**: to the considerable sum of

Explanations

Caption: red deer (n.): Originating from Europe they were introduced into New Zealand in 1861. Without natural enemies their population flourished and led to problems of overgrazing. They were domesticated and have been commercially farmed since 1969. In 1998 New Zealand Red Deer Farming generated 185,000,000 NZ $ worth of export business.

Info

New Zealand's economy

New Zealand's small economy is heavily dependent on overseas trade. Traditionally, a large proportion of New Zealand's exports, mainly agricultural products, went to the United Kingdom. In the past 20 years, however, New Zealand has adapted to a changing world so that Asia is now more dominant. The largest merchandise export markets are Australia, USA and Japan. New Zealand has developed its agriculture and manufacturing industries to suit the needs of niche markets. This has meant that New Zealand has moved away from its dependence on dairy, meat and wool exports as forestry, horticulture, fishing, manufacturing and tourism have become more significant.

Awareness

1 Which products from New Zealand can you buy in German shops?

Comprehension

2 How did New Zealand's relationship to Europe and especially Britain change after 1973?
3 What did New Zealand's policy focus on in the 1980s?
4 In which way do both New Zealand and European countries profit from an economic partnership?

Analysis

5 Throughout his speech McKinnon uses metaphorical expressions. Find out where he uses them and explain them in their context.
6 One of these metaphors illustrates an important principle of New Zealand's economic policy. Show that New Zealand's recent trade relations reflect this principle.

Opinion

7 New Zealand is a member of APEC (Asia Pacific Economic Cooperation Forum). This membership is a matter of controversial discussion. Why do you think might people oppose a membership in such an organisation?
8 Later in his speech McKinnon looks ahead and speaks of far-reaching decisions to be made view of political alignments and ethnic conflicts. Which changes have happened since he made this speech in 1996?

Project

9 Look up the OECD statistics on the internet and find out the figures which characterise the economic performance of a country. On the basis of these statistics compare the economic performance of Australia, New Zealand and Germany over the last three years. Present your findings in the form of graphs and diagrams.

23

John Arlidge

"Fans flock to New Zealand's Tolkien trail"

Tourism has always been an important part of New Zealand's economy. At present one in ten jobs is related to this industry which contributes $15 billion (9.1%) to the GDP. In the last two decades the number of visitors to New Zealand has increased every year, even during years of worldwide recession. In 2009 two and a half million people came to "God Zone", a country which has a lot more to offer than 45 million sheep, e.g. 3000 glaciers, hundreds of mountain peaks higher than 7500 feet, untouched forests and cristal-clear lakes. That is why, traditionally, most tourists come to enjoy the beautiful landscape and take part in nature-based activities such as scenic trips, trekking, bush walks or wildlife and adventure activities. In 2002 New Zealand's tourism industry added one more attraction to its list of activities: visiting movie locations, especially those of Peter Jackson's *Lord of the Rings*. - John Arlidge, "Fans flock to New Zealand's Tolkien trail", *The Observer*, Sunday 6 January 2002.

For years it has been the butt of bad jokes about sheep, lager and more sheep. Now, thanks to a bunch of elves, orcs and hobbits, New Zealand has shrugged off its dull image to become one of this year's most fashionable tourist destinations.

The £300 million blockbuster *The Lord of the Rings* – in which the scenery of North and South Island was used to evoke Tolkien's mystical Middle Earth – has sparked an unprecedented rise in holiday bookings. Leading operators say sales have risen by more than 20 per cent in the two weeks since the film was released. They predict visitor numbers will double by the end of the year.

Specialist tour firm Bridge the World says its £1,529 'Follow the Fellowship of the Ring' tour, which takes visitors on a 12-night tour of sites used in the film, is selling twice as fast as expected. James Bell, the firm's marketing director, said: 'The film has had a rapid impact. People want to see the land behind the movie.'

The London-based New Zealand Affair, which tailor-makes £2,000 packages for Tolkien fans, said the telephones began ringing the moment the film was released. 'It's a case of "read the book, seen the movie, now get the holiday", 'said Tim Stubbings, a spokesman for the firm. 'It's a little too soon for accurate figures, but I would say inquiries are up at least 20 per cent.

'The film is a wonderful advertisement. People see it and then call up the next day wanting to visit the places they've seen on screen, so we've put together a number of special packages to suggest the best routes to see both film locations and New Zealand's famous sights.'

Most tourists start with what has been dubbed the 'Tolkien trail' in Auckland, before heading off to the coast. The most popular destinations are Tongariro national park, which became the dark land of Mordor, Glenorchy and Lake Wakatipu, which were used to evoke the magic woodland of Lothlorien, and the Queenstown region, home of Tolkien's Misty Mountains, the Summit of Amon Hen and Ford of Bruinen. A 'map of Middle Earth' directs obsessive Tolkien fans to the exact spots where their favourite characters stood.

Robert Doyle, 39, a father of two from Bedford who has just booked to travel to New Zealand in March, said: 'I'd always planned to go to New Zealand but never got round to it. It just seemed such a long way to go with two days' jet lag there and back.

New Zealand visitors 1999–2008 (in millions)	
1999	1.52
2000	1.65
2001	1.85
2002	1.95
2003	2.01
2004	2.12
2005	2.37
2006	2.38
2007	2.45
2008	2.50

Source: New Zealand Ministry of Tourism (NZMT), http://www.tourism.govt.nz/

'I loved *The Hobbit* and *The Lord of the Rings* and when I saw the film I spent the whole time looking at the scenery. I'd never seen anything like it. I booked up last week. I know Tolkien wrote the whole thing in Worcestershire but New Zealand seems much more exciting.'

Visitors are also being attracted by the good exchange rates – the NZ dollar has depreciated by as much as 10 per cent against the pound over the past 15 months – and the sharp drop in air fares. A return air ticket now costs on average £550, which is less than half the price two years ago.

Travel experts say the *Lord of the Rings* effect could be just the boost New Zealand's tourist industry needs. One told The Observer: 'New Zealand has historically had an image problem. To put it bluntly, people have seen it as the dullest place on earth with more sheep than people. The more people go on the Tolkien trail, go trekking, go bungee-jumping and visit the winelands and come back and tell their friends how good it was, the better.'

There are two sequels to *The Lord of the Rings*: *The Fellowship of the Ring*. One will be released next Christmas and the other in 2003. Tourist chiefs estimate that over the three years the film will boost New Zealand's tourism industry by one third. Geoff Kearsley, an expert in tourism at Otago University, said: 'If this film achieves half of what is expected, it will be massive for New Zealand.'

Back in the UK demand from the notoriously obsessive Tolkien fans is creating some unusual problems for holiday firms. 'We like to say anything is possible, but some requests are proving a little too, well, fictional,' said Tim Stubbings. 'We're scratching our heads on how we can provide accommodation at Bag End, and just how do you tell someone the Mines of Moria live in the director's computer?'

Scene from The Fellowship of the Ring

Vocabulary

Intro: GDP (n.): Gross Domestic Product, i.e. the total value of all goods and services produced in a country, in one year, except for income received from abroad – **1 butt** (n.): here: target – **3 to shrug s.th. off** (v.): to treat s.th. as unimportant and not worry about it – **19f. to tailor-make** (v.): to make perfectly suitable for s.o. – **59 to boost** (v.): to increase or improve s.th. and make it more successful

Explanations

Intro: God Zone (infml.): local for New Zealand which is regarded as God's Own Country – **84 Bag End** (n.): a hobbit hole, the comfortable home of Bilbo Baggins, a character in *The Lord of the Rings* – **85 Moria** (n.): a vast underground complex in the mountains of Middle Earth in the same novel and films

Awareness

1 Consult New Zealand's Ministry of Tourism website and find out the main reasons why people visit this country.
2 Which are the most important places of action in *The Lord of the Rings*? Give a short description of each of these places.

Comprehension

3 What image do most people traditionally have of New Zealand?
4 Describe the reaction of travel agencies to this new tourist attraction.
5 How do Tolkien fans spend their holidays in the country?
6 Apart from the beautiful landscape and the movie locations – why might tourists visit this country?
7 Why were the travel agencies unable to fulfil all the visitors' requests?

Analysis

8 What does Arlidge contend and which evidence does he give to support his contention?
9 What did travel experts expect to be the effect of the films? Evaluate their estimates on the basis of the figures given in the table on p. 63.

Opinion

10 There are always two sides of the medal. The article only presents a positive view of an increase in tourist numbers. What do you think are the dangers New Zealand must be aware of?
In this context experts speak of "Disneyland" and of "sustainable tourism". What do they refer to?

Project

11 Find out which other "blockbuster" movies were filmed in New Zealand and write a short guide to the most spectacular movie locations of the country.

Competence Training

You can use this Viewfinder volume to practise most or all of the skills you will need to satisfy the requirements set out in the European Frame of Reference (up to level C1) and tested in exams like the German *Abitur* (all *Bundesländer*), TOEFL and IELTS.

Details about the skills (often referred to in German as *Kompetenzen*) that you can work to improve, and which of the texts and/or sections from the book will be most useful in doing it are set out on these pages. They provide cross-references to the Viewfinder Reference Library (where you can find out exactly how to do things). You will get the RL from your teacher or you can download it from http://www.langenscheidt.de. At the end there is a revision checklist to make sure you can remember the main points the book deals with. This can be used for exam revision.

Language skills

Basic and advanced language skills	Oral skills	Written skills
• grammar/structure • vocabulary (new words, word formation) • idiom • register	• pronunciation • intonation • presentation	• spelling • punctuation • text layout

All the texts in this book can help you practise and extend your competence in the active language skills of **speaking** and **writing** and the receptive skills of **reading** and **listening**. You should have learnt the basic language skills in English before you started working with this book. If you're not very confident yet, don't worry. You'll be able to practise all these skills and bring them up to a more advanced level working with any of the texts here. Some of tasks are better for oral skills and others for written skills. Try to learn new words in their contexts (without trying to find the equivalent in your own language), and note down points which give you trouble, concentrating on learning them and checking your work specially to make sure you don't make the same mistake again. You will find a lot of helpful material in the Reference Library.

Speaking
- ability to pronounce English correctly (using correct accent and intonation)
- ability to use different idioms, registers
- managing discourse (making an appropriate choice of vocabulary, sentence structure, rhetorical devices, text structure) in, for example, everyday conversation or presentations

Reading
- comprehension of content
- understanding of a writer's train of thought
- ability to recognise and understand a variety of text types, fictional and non-fictional

Listening
- comprehension of content
- ability to understand a variety of spoken text types (unscripted conversations, discussions; scripted news broadcasts, talks, speeches)
- being aware of rhetorical devices used by speakers
- ability to understand different social and geographical accents and dialects

Writing
- ability to spell and punctuate correctly
- ability to write a number of different text types (essay, letter, report, presentation, commentary, analysis) using the appropriate vocabulary, grammar and text structure.

Don't forget: you can learn from mistakes, but repeated mistakes are a waste of time. The more proficient your English is, the more fun it will be to use, and the better impression it will make on your communication partners.

Text types

This volume contains the following types of non-fictional and fictional texts which you will be asked to analyse.

non-fictional texts	
newspaper report	texts 17, 23
newspaper comment	texts 15, 17, 23
bar chart	text 16
table	texts 11, 14, 23
historical text	texts 1, 7, 8, 10, 19, 20
speech	texts 3, 20, 22
academic article	text 11
diary	text 1
internet presentation	text 12
chart	texts 5 (p. 19), 23
questionnaire	text 12
fictional texts	
myth	text 5
novel	text 2
short story	text 4
drama	text 21
poem	text 6
pop song	texts 9, 13; p. 5
visual texts	
photographs	texts 2, 3, 4, 5, 9, 10, 11, 13, 14, 15, 16, 17, 20, 22, 23; p. 4f., 52f.
paintings, engravings	text 5, 7, 8, 10
maps	text 19, Australia p. 4, New Zealand p. 52
wanted poster	text 10

Particular study skills when approaching texts

Tasks and Questions

The tasks and questions which follow each text are designed to develop skills and competences in a number of areas: language practice and understanding, analysing and appreciating a wide variety of fictional and non-fictional texts. The tasks will also enable you to develop your own ideas on the topics dealt with, and motivate you to carry out further research into areas that interest you.

Awareness:

Before reading a text you should be aware of certain ideas, facts, expectations or prejudices which form the context of the text itself. Skills to practise here include:

note-taking: this is a key skill in a) preparing for discussions and b) reading and analysing texts (see below)	all texts

Collecting and collating ideas:

brainstorming	texts 1 (2), 5 (2), 7 (1), 9 (1, 2, 3), 12 (1), 14 (3)
mindmapping	text 4 (1)
question and answer session	text 4 (7)
reports on individual experience	texts 1 (1), 11 (2), 12 (1), 20 (1), 22 (1)
general discussion	texts 3 (9), 6 (9), 11 (12), 14 (5)

library research	texts 1, 2 (11), 3 (11), 8, 10 (1), 13 (9)
internet research	texts 1, 2 (1), 3 (2, 10, 11), 4, 5, 7, 9 (9), 10 (1), 11 (11, 12), 12 (9–13), 14 (6–11),16 (8, 10), 17 (1, 9), 23 (1, 11)
interpretation of figures, tables and charts	texts 11 (8, 13), 14 (1, 2), 23 (9)
role-play	text 1 (6), 3 (8), 16 (9)

DURING READING YOU CAN PRACTISE A NUMBER OF SKILLS:

- skimming for general impressions
- scanning to find out facts or information
- note-taking (RL A 4)
- marking important passages
- deducing meanings from context
- using a monolingual dictionary (RL A 3)
- using a bilingual dictionary (RL A 3)
- dividing the text
- summarising (RL C 3)
- finding the deeper meaning
- appreciating aesthetic qualities

In this Viewfinder volume you can practise all these skills on any text. Usually, apart from skimming, you will need to read a text at least three times. The questions under the heading 'Comprehension' are designed for the first eight skills on the list; the 'Analysis' questions will help you practise the last three skills.

AFTER READING:

After you have read the text there are 'Analysis' and 'Opinion' questions to help you discover more meaning in the text, and think about what it means for you personally or what its implications are. You can do these questions alone, in pairs or groups, or as a class. You can answer them individually, present your answers to a plenum, or present them in writing.

Individual written answers can be in the form of clearly organised notes or an essay.
Individual oral answers can be in the form of a presentation based on notes.
Make sure your answers are clear and concise and relevant.
Check that your listeners have understood your answer.

Answers can also be produced orally or in writing in pair-work or group-work. This will enable you to practise the following teamwork skills:

- using the opportunity of practising English without being supervised
- organising and dividing up tasks
- co-operating and pooling ideas and skills
- using appropriate research tools
- practising time-management skills (keeping to a timetable)
- choosing an appropriate type of presentation
- using media as presentation aids.

The 'Opinion' questions can be used for various forms of discussion, argument or debate.
These can be used to practise oral communication skills (see RL B 2). The following tasks are particularly suitable: texts 3 (9), 4 (9), 6 (9), 12, 14 (5), 17 (8)

Textual analysis skills

The text analysis questions form the core of your coursework in English in the *Oberstufe* and their aim is to help you

a) work out what meanings the text might have for you and other readers
b) discover how the text affects you and the means used to achieve this
c) make judgments and write about the content of the text, its value, and its relevance to you.

NON-FICTIONAL TEXTS:

establishing types of text (RL C 1.2.1.)	e.g. texts 1 (diary), 3 (speech), 14 (survey)
content (fact v. opinion etc) (RL C 1.2.1.)	texts 3, 14 (4), 16
structure and form (RL C 1.2.1.)	texts 1 (5), 3 (5)
function (RL C 1.2.2.)	text 3 (7)
style and tone (RL C 1.2.2.)	texts 3 (6), 8 (4)
integrating visual components	pp. 4f.
genre (RL C 1.2)	texts 1 (diary), 3, 20, 22 (speech)
theme (RL C 1.2)	text 17 (6)
character and characterisation (RL C 1.2)	texts 10 (5), 15 (3)
setting and atmosphere (RL C 1.2)	text 3 (6)

FICTIONAL TEXTS:

establishing types of text (RL C 1.1)	e.g. texts 2, 5, 6
style and tone (RL C 1.1)	texts 2 (5, 8), 4 (4), 6 (7), 9 (6)
recognizing humour and irony	texts 6, 9
genre (RL C 1.1.)	p. 5 (folk song), texts 2 (historical novel), 4 (short story), 5 (myth), 6 (poem), 9, 13 (song), 21 (drama)
theme (RL C 1.1.)	texts 6 (2, 8), 13 (6)
character and characterisation (RL C 1.1.)	texts 2 (2), 9 (4), 21 (4, 9)
setting and atmosphere (RL C 1.1.)	text 2 (5)
structure and formal aspects (RL C 1.1.)	texts 2 (8), 4 (4), 5 (7), 6 (4), 13 (4)

Listening comprehension skills

Any of the texts can be used for listening comprehension if you listen to someone reading them, make notes and answer questions or summarize the text. In this context, speeches are particularly relevant because they are delivered publicly and the intonation will often imply the speaker's overall goal. Watching film scenes will also test listening comprehension skills. If the speaker is a non-native speaker of English (e.g. a first-generation Indian immigrant to the UK), his pronunciation and intonation may differ from standard British English.

Texts that are particularly useful in this context are:	texts 3, 22 (internet recordings)
Texts and music	Australia p. 5, texts 9, 13

Visual text comprehension skills

Analysing photographs	pp. 4f., 52f.
Analysing film	text 3 (12)
Analysing a painting	text 5

Particular writing skills / creative writing skills

that you can practise in 'Projects' or on the whole text:

Essay	any text
Paper	any text
Letter	texts 12 (1), 13 (10), 16 (7)
Legal text	texts 5 (15, 16), 15 (8)
Guide	texts 4 (1), 14 (3), 23 (11)
Script	text 10 (9)
Newspaper article	text 10 (8)

Intercultural Skills

Intercultural linguistic skills: When you use another language you need intercultural skills. This is because languages do not just have different words; they differ fundamentally in the ways they express thoughts, or even sometimes in the thoughts they choose to express. So there is no such thing as word-for-word or exact translation. Just think, e.g., of the differences between the German word *fahren* and the English word *drive*. Or where, in German, you might write: "Mit diesem Bild will der Autor die Unmenschlichkeit des Krieges ausdrücken.", in English we might say "The author uses this image to express the horrors of war."

So when working with this book you need to develop skills in relation to the use of the foreign language:

- **Intercultural linguistic awareness:** e.g. seeing how differently words and structures are used in English from their 'equivalents' in your language;
- **Intercultural linguistic competence:** e.g. being able to use the foreign language in the way that members of that language community use and understand it;
- **Register and tone:** e.g. being able to recognize and use different registers like academic or colloquial, or different tones like serious, humorous or sarcastic.

All the texts and tasks in this volume expect you to work in the medium of English, which will help you to practise these vital skills.

Specifically, you may be required to actively use various types of equivalents between English and your own language. This will involve the following skills:

- **Translation** (German: Übersetzung): Here you must try to find the nearest possible written equivalent in the other language while making sure that it reads like an original text in terms of structure, idiom, register and tone. This is particularly difficult in literary texts where you have to think of the aesthetic effect as well.
- **Interpreting** (German: dolmetschen): As an interpreter you must try to give the nearest equivalent possible of someone's spoken words, either after they have said them, or simultaneously.
- **Conveying the sense** (German: Mediation): People may want to know the sense, or message, of a document. They need to know the important facts and figures, but the particular linguistic expressions used in the original are irrelevant.

The texts (or extracts from them) in this Viewfinder volume which are most suitable for translating or conveying the sense are texts 1, 5, 10. You could also convey the sense of particular positions, like those of the characters in texts 3, 11, 15. For a real challenge you could try to describe the Aboriginal belief of Dreamtime.
In addition, this Viewfinder volume *Australia and New Zealand Down Under On Top* also deals specifically with the interactions of different cultures, and so is particularly useful for practising other intercultural skills.

Two forms of intercultural awareness in particular are being addressed and introduced in this volume.

First, the volume teaches students to be aware of similarities and differences between a non-Western culture (Aboriginal culture) and a Western culture (England, Ireland).
Secondly, Australia (and to a certain extent New Zealand) is introduced as a multi-ethnic nation, with many ethnic, religious and linguistic communities negotiating with each other (intercultural awareness within Australia as a nation).

Intercultural awareness and familiarization	texts 1, 2, 4, 5, 8, 14, 18, 19, 20, 21
Indigenous culture	texts 1, 2, 3, 4, 5, 6, 9, 20, 21
Empathizing with others	texts 2, 3, 4, 5, 21
Socio-historical contexts	British colonialism in Australia: texts 1, 2, 8; crime: text 1, 7, 10; different modes of schooling: text 12
Contemporary problems	texts 4, 6, 9, 14, 21 (inter-ethnic conflict), 5, 13, 17 (ecology), 14 (immigration), 15 (republicanism), 16, 17 (climate change/greenhouse emissions), 21 (multiculturalism)

Particular texts will give information about intercultural topics:

National unity and identity	texts 3, 14, 20
Language and dialect	texts 2, 6, 9
Cultural assumptions and particularities	texts 1, 2, 5, 9, 11, 15
Religion	text 5
Globalisation	texts 22, 23
Gender Issues	texts 1 (9), 8, 11
Poverty	text 7
Prejudices and stereotypes	texts 2, 4, 6, 9, 21
School systems	text 12
Integration and equality	texts 3, 6, 13
Conflicts and reactions	texts 2, 3, 10, 20, 21

Revision

As preparation for exams and assessments, it is a good idea to revise the main points you've learnt in this *Viewfinder*. The information may be useful if you are asked questions about this topic, or as background knowledge to put other things into context. And if you are sure about these points it will boost your confidence.

Key terms and concepts

ethnic diversity	from ethnic minorities to super-diversity	Who is there in Australia?
identity	according to ethnic origin hyphenated identity	Who are they?
immigrant/migrant		'push' and 'pull' factors
member of ethnic group/refugee/asylum seeker economic migrant		
integration assimilation segregation	'two-way street' (equality)	influencing one another adopting 'host' identity leading separate lives
xenophobia racism		hatred of foreigners
discrimination	to discriminate against s.o.	in housing, employment
prejudice stereotype		unjustified ideas
legislation positive action	anti-discrimination legislation (v. affirmative action, positive discrimination)	
political correctness	PC	

Basic terms that are intertwined with Australia

Aboriginals	
Australian-ness	("Aussie"; bush/hinterland/Outback; damper; fair dinkum; stockman; pioneer; convicts; outdoor activities; matilda; mate)
Commonwealth	
Dreamtime	
mateship	
penal colony	
tourism	
reconciliation	
Stolen Generation	

Contents of Reference Library